# Books YOUR Kids WILL Talk About!

BY

## Susan Hepler
## & Maria Salvadore

nea
NATIONAL EDUCATION ASSOCIATION
www.nea.org
**Great Public Schools for Every Child**

N E A   P R O F E S S I O N A L   L I B R A R Y

**Printing History**
First Printing: June 2003

Note: The opinions in this publication should not be construed as representing the policy or position of the National Education Association. Materials published by the NEA Professional Library are intended to be discussion documents for educators who are concerned with specialized interests of the profession.

**Credits:** *Front Cover Design:* Eun Ju Cho. *Back Cover Illustration*: Adjoa J. Burrowes. *Back Cover Design*: Eun Ju Cho. *Book Design:* Groff Creative, Inc. *Editors:* Sabrina Holcomb and Sarah Larson. *Editorial Assistants:* Marcus Brock, Lorinda Bullock, Leah Lakins, and Mary Kershaw.

**Library of Congress Cataloging-in-Publication Data**
Hepler, Susan Ingrid.
    Books your kids will talk about!: a guide to children's literature for teachers and parents/
by Susan Hepler and Maria Salvadore.
        p. cm.
    ISBN 0-8106-2051-0
    1. Children—Books and reading—United States. 2. Children's literature—Stories, plots, etc.  3. Child psychology—Juvenile literature—Bibliography. 4. Bibliotherapy for children.
I. Salvadore, Maria.  II. Title.

Z1037.H49 2003
028.5'5—dc21

2003053978

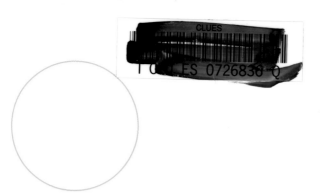

# Dedication

To our children, Nicky, Andrew, and Emily, who teach us so much when we talk about books.

# Acknowledgements

As we wrote *Books Your Kids Will Talk About,* our thinking was constantly influenced by the many teachers, librarians, parents, booksellers, and publishers with whom we have talked over the decades. We are deeply indebted to them for sharing their enthusiasm for books, for telling us stories of the children with whom they work and whom they love, and for putting books in our hands that we "just have to read." As we talked about what books we would include in our annotations, we recalled lively discussions that made certain books come alive for us and remain vivid in our memories. Those are the books that have made it into this one.

We specifically wish to express our gratitude to our longtime mentors, Charlotte S. Huck, formerly at the Ohio State University and now living in Redlands, California, and Anne MacLeod, University of Maryland, College Park. Their good professional example and insights into children and literature were the catalysts that spurred us to joyfully undertake lifelong careers in the service of children's books. Thanks for launching us and providing necessary rebooting over the years. Special thanks also are due to Regie Routman, who has been a generous-spirited inspiration, a source of great wisdom in the field of reading, and a great support in our own professional development.

Numerous colleagues have shared ideas and books with us. We have benefited immensely from Jewell Stoddard, Politics and Prose Bookstore in Washington, D.C., whose unerring eye for quality, encyclopedic memory, and far-ranging knowledge of children's books have guided us on many occasions. Ann Van Deusen, librarian at Burgundy Farm Country Day School, Alexandria, Virginia, always stands ready to suggest a book (or a dozen) to explore particular themes and ideas. Susan Steinberg, George Mason Elementary School, Alexandria, Virginia, has throughout the years graciously shared thoughtful comments on books evoked from the fourth and fifth graders she teaches. And a book this far-ranging would not be possible without the dialogue provided by our colleagues in Capitol Choices and in

The Children's Book Guild of Washington, D.C. We continue to marvel at the depth, breadth, and joy in books that we discover in the presence of these friends.

We owe a debt of gratitude to Sabrina Holcomb, at the National Education Association (NEA), who originally conceived of this book, believed in our abilities, and who shepherded it through its many phases. Special thanks to Anita Merina and Michelle Green, also at NEA, whose creativity and commitment to children's literature and its creators added much to this book. We're also grateful to the educators and parents who shared their stories with us and to NEA's Read Across America Advisory Board for reviewing our manuscript.

Kudos to Sarah Larson, our capable developmental editor, for her care and belief in this project. We are indebted to her for her intelligent and thoughtful comments and her tenacity in helping to realize this book's vision. Also, a special thanks to Darcy Bradley, Bellingham, Washington, who took time from her own writing to provide valuable insights at a crucial time.

We are grateful that Union Station's food court was noisy enough to accommodate our enthusiastic and wonderful planning meetings. It became our unofficial office as we worked our way through piles of books and resources. And as always, our thanks to our patient husbands, who provide unflagging support for our many book projects and enthusiasms.

Maria Salvadore and Susan Hepler
Washington, D.C.
May 2003

# About the Authors

**SUSAN HEPLER, Ph.D.**, is a children's literature specialist who lives in Alexandria, Virginia. She has taught elementary, high school, college, and graduate students about children's literature for over 30 years. She is an active member of The Children's Book Guild of Washington, D.C, and served both as president and chair of the Washington Post/ Children's Book Guild Nonfiction Award. An author of the widely used college textbook, *Children's Literature in the Elementary School, 8th ed.* (McGraw-Hill, 2004), she has also designed and written curriculum guides for public television, children's books, and school districts. In addition to writing articles about children's literature, Susan reviews children's books for *School Library Journal* and the online database, Children's Literature Comprehensive Database (CLCD) service. She currently speaks to groups about the power of children's books to raise excited and thoughtful readers.

**MARIA SALVADORE** now works as a children's literature specialist, consulting with local and national organizations. Before becoming a consultant, she served as Coordinator of Children's Services for the District of Columbia Public Library system. Prior to her return to Washington, Maria worked as the Children's Services Coordinator in the Cambridge (MA) Public Library. While there, she worked with the Center for the Study of Children's Literature at Simmons College. Maria teaches graduate level courses in children's literature at the University of Maryland. Maria has reviewed books for *Appraisal Science Books*, *Horn Book Guide,* and *The Horn Book Magazine,* and continues to review for *School Library Journal.* She was consulting editor and contributor to *The Essential Guide to Children's Books and Their Creators* (Houghton Mifflin, 2002) and contributed to *Children's Books and Their Creators* (Houghton Mifflin, 1995), both edited by Anita Silvey. Maria has served on or chaired various award juries including the Boston Globe–Horn Book Awards, the Caldecott Medal, and the Washington Post–Children's Book Guild Nonfiction Award.

# Contributors

 **Michelle Y. Green** is a writer/editor in the **NEA Human and Civil Rights** department. A graduate of the Johns Hopkins University master's program in writing, Michelle's biography, *A Strong Right Arm: The Story of Mamie "Peanut" Johnson*, is a 2003 Notable Social Studies Trade Book for Young People.

 **Barbara Kapinus** is a senior policy analyst and reading consultant in the **NEA Student Achievement** department. Barbara has been Director of the Curriculum and Instructional Improvement Program at the Council of Chief State School Officers and Specialist for Reading and Communication Skills at the Maryland State Department of Education. She has also published articles and book chapters on a range of reading-related topics.

 **Anita Merina** is a writer/editor in the **NEA External Partnerships and Advocacy** department. One of the coordinators of NEA's Read Across America Program, she is also a minority community outreach liaison and a contributor to *NEA Today* magazine. Anita, editor of *Philippine-American Short Stories*, is currently writing a children's book about Olympic diver Victoria Manalo Draves.

# Contents

# THE BUZZ ABOUT BOOKS

A second grader slogged through all 734 pages of *Harry Potter and the Goblet of Fire* by J.K. Rowling (Scholastic, 2000) because he wanted to find out what happened. He also wanted to keep up with his older siblings who kept talking about the good parts of the story. This same child exclaimed "Oh, good!" when he learned the book's sequel would have at least the same number of pages.

On a recent visit to a kindergarten class, we met a group of children who could identify all their favorite monsters by name in *Dinosaurs! The Biggest, Baddest, Strangest, Fastest* by Howard Zimmerman (Atheneum, 2000). They eagerly shared their knowledge (and the really gory pictures) with each other and with the adults in the classroom.

Before she visited her favorite uncle, a sixth-grade girl read *Time* magazine from cover to cover to talk the politics of the day with him.

Why were these children so highly motivated to read? Why were they so eager to tackle materials considered difficult for their ages? It's no secret that the ability to read is one of the key factors for a child's success in school and beyond. But to read, children need more than an understanding of the way language works; they need to be motivated. So, what inspires a child to turn off the TV, shut off the video game, and pick up a book?

## Talking About Books

Motivation is as varied as the reader, but the eager readers described here had two significant things in common: They had discovered the allure of reading and the thrill of talking about what they'd read. Each child had discovered that books can be magical, especially when shared. And each child had someone they could talk to about what they'd read—either other children or a caring adult.

Part of what makes a book fun and memorable for adults is talking about it. Kids are no different. And, in addition to the pleasure of discussion, talking about books is a powerful tool for learning. Talk deepens thinking. Scientists now agree that brain development continues well into adolescence. What young people notice and talk about can actually create new neural pathways. Conversation can help children find meaning in what they read as they look at pictures, find words, and notice things that other readers point out.

Conversation is also the cornerstone for a solid relationship between children and the adults who live and work with them—parents, teachers, librarians, and other significant grownups. Books provide a connection, a way to talk about ideas in a neutral, non-threatening way. It may be easier for a child to discuss what one character did to anger the other in Rebecca Jones' *Matthew and Tilly*—and how the friends resolved it—than for the child to consider his or her own bad behavior. Children who discuss the courage it takes for two boys to make friends in *Yo! Yes?* by Chris Raschka may view making new playground friendships in a new light. A child who reads about the neighborhood Kam Mak describes in *My*

### Can I **Read** It When you're **Done?**

As four children get ready for silent reading, they're anything but silent. "I'm almost done with my book. It's sooo good," says one. Looking over at the title, another offers, "Oh yeah, *Holes*. I read that, too. I liked it when he discovers the lipstick case with K.B. The whole story was like a big puzzle and it all fit together at the end." The third reader adds, "Hey, they made a movie out of that book, you know. I'm going to see it with my Dad," while the last reader asks, "Can I read it when you're done?"

**SUSAN STEINBERG**
LANGUAGE ARTS/READING TEACHER
GEORGE MASON ELEMENTARY SCHOOL
ALEXANDRIA, VIRGINIA

*Chinatown: One Year in Poems* may see how families and friends are similar against a backdrop of cultural differences.

Because talking about books is so important, we've tried to introduce children's books that spark thought and discussion about ideas of interest to both children and adults. These dialogues can take place as formal classroom discussions or informal conversations between adults and children at home, in the car, on a walk, or in a community center. The conversations can be lengthy or just shared snippets of an idea in passing.

The books we've selected give readers from kindergarten to sixth grade, with varied backgrounds and different interests, lots to connect with and talk about. When eight-year-old Keith was having a tough time with the kids at school about being adopted, he was able to see himself and his family in Liz Rosenberg's *We Wanted You*. This book assured Keith and his parents that there were others who'd had a similar experience.

Often children will want to talk about the child at the center of the story, how he or she solves a problem and makes choices. Books can motivate adults to talk about these issues, too. Denise, an incarcerated mother enrolled in a prison family literacy program, felt empowered to tell her story to her daughter when she read *Tell Me A Story, Mama*, by Angela Johnson, in preparation for her daughter's visit. This book started a dialogue between Denise and her child that extended into the school. The girl was able to tell her teacher that her mother was in prison when the teacher shared her copy of *Tell Me a Story, Mama* with the class.

Conversations about books are not meant to be "bibliotherapy." A child who has just lost a pet may or may not want to read about it. But a child who has a stockpile of shared books has some knowledge to draw on and other ways to respond to life

## That's Me!

When my son's classmates started noticing that Keith didn't look like either of us, Keith told them he was adopted. One child told my son that we were only his temporary foster parents. "One day," he said, "your 'real' parents will come back to get you." That night, a miserable Keith curled up beside me as I read aloud from *We Wanted You* by Liz Rosenberg, an adoption story told from the parents' perspective. "We weren't your first father and mother. But we waited for you...and that's how you know that you are really ours. Because we were yours, all along." When he heard me read these words, Keith shrieked "That's me!"

ALEX FISCHER
Parent of an 8-Year-Old

experiences. Children who've talked about Vera B. Williams' *A Chair for My Mother* will be more receptive to the helping community around them. Those who've read and talked about the resilient Angel in Katherine Paterson's *Same Stuff as Stars* may see their own troubles in a new light. Books can build empathy, promote understanding, and provide kids with the adventure or poignancy of vicarious experiences.

## Why These Books?

We've never been in an age with such rich children's books. State-of-the-art printing techniques, luscious art commingling with text, and nontraditional styles are just part of the reason. Today's children's books also contain an amazing diversity and range of themes.

The books included in the following chapters were chosen for their overall quality and staying power, either proven or potential. And they present age-appropriate themes in ways that are intriguing and lively. We've drawn on lists of notable books, award winners, and parents' and teachers' choices, as well as on our extensive experience in working with children, adults, and books.

The books we've selected are those most likely to be embraced by children and to inspire open discussion. And since children's books enjoyed only by children are not always the best books, we've included children's books that adults can honestly celebrate reading and will want to find time to talk about with the children in their lives.

Children return to books that have universal themes and are well presented, no matter when they were published. While about half of the selected books were published within the last five years, some are modern classics. Only the original copyright date is included with the bibliographic information. Other editions may be available for purchase or through libraries. Most of the books we've recommended are in print, but the few that aren't should be widely available in schools or public libraries.

We've recommended some highly pictorial books for middle and upper grade students, with a wide range of artistic styles. These books provide a wonderful opportunity for adults and children to discuss how ideas are presented in text and illustration and the relationship between images and words. Together adults and children can slow down to look carefully and see what's on the page before them, how the story unfolds, or how the pictures extend the words. Today's illustrators use all sorts of materials from paint or colored pencils to torn cloth, collage, beads, and even dyed paper pulp poured through a screen. One of the first things a reader often asks is "How did they make the pictures?"

Picture books have become increasingly sophisticated. They allow readers to look carefully at how and why pictures create a certain impression or have a particular impact. Talking about images in books teaches kids to take a harder, more critical look at the other images in their world.

## Literature To Go

It's a fact that when parents team up with teachers, everyone wins. Students get the reinforcement they need outside of the classroom (which makes my job easier), and they get to spend quality time with their parents. At my school, the kindergarten teachers send "traveling literature bags" home with the kids. We put five books in a bag, each dealing with a specific theme or author for the family to focus on. Every night, parents read a book from the bag to their child. This ritual has become so popular with our students, they get upset with us if we skip a week. We've gotten such great results, the first-grade teachers rave about our former students and how they're well ahead of their peers when they enter the class.

**COLLEEN HART**
KINDERGARTEN TEACHER
KEOTA ELEMENTARY SCHOOL
KEOTA, IOWA

Nicky, a fourth grader, has talked about the images in Steven Kellogg's books ever since he was in kindergarten. Nicky and his mom have spent many hours sharing Kellogg's books and discussing how the artist presented his stories through pictures and words. (And there are many stories in Kellogg's art—the story that goes along with the words, the side stories, and the asides from the characters.) As a result, Nicky's expressive skills have been enhanced by interpreting and talking about illustrations, the way pictures and words work together in books, and the ideas that each conveys. Like Nicky's mom, we've tried to select books that keep readers coming back to them, books that have keen visual interest, and also books that will withstand multiple readings.

## What's Inside This Book

The books we've chosen are organized around ten themes that are especially germane to a child's world. Each of the ten chapters begins with a brief discussion of the theme and includes interviews with authors and illustrators and inspiring anecdotes from teachers, parents, and other adults who work with children.

- **Living in a Family (Chapter 1)** explores how families are created, how they live, work, play, share sadness, and also celebrate together.

- Next to home, school is usually the second most influential environment in a child's life. **Going to School (Chapter 2)** examines the myriad joys and challenges children experience as they learn and grow with their school family.

- **Making Friends (Chapter 3)** takes a look at the impact of friendships, how friendships are created, what it means to be a friend, and a few delightfully unusual friendships.

- Schools create one community but so do neighborhoods. How kids relate and connect to the various communities in which they live, work, and play is explored in **Connecting to Communities (Chapter 4)**.

- Diverse communities build our diverse world. **Looking at the World (Chapter 5)** provides kids with a global perspective of various cultures and traditions though many areas of the world.

- While children look outward to discover their world, they're also learning about self-discovery. **Looking in a Mirror (Chapter 6)** introduces readers to real and imagined children and adults who explore the thrills and challenges of growing up.

- There's something about shared laughter that's especially delightful. Humor can be a wonderful way to learn about ourselves and connect with others. **Laughing Together (Chapter 7)** explores what makes readers laugh at different ages with different senses of humor.

- Humor can help us get through tough times. But difficulties are so varied and kids confront so many as they grow, they need reminders that things will get better. Hope is a common theme—along with others, of course—in **Getting Through Tough Times (Chapter 8)**.

- Kids are empowered to change some part of their world when they hear about others who've made positive changes in their own lives. Both biographical and fictional stories in **Making A Difference (Chapter 9)** depict young people as well as adults who, in small ways and large, make an impact on the world in which they live.

- The final chapter is really a beginning. **Exploring Imagination (Chapter 10)** introduces the impact of creativity and imagination on all aspects of a child's life, from inspired inventions to fantastical "what-ifs."

Within each of these thematic chapters, books are organized by title, and recommended for primary, intermediate, and/or upper grade children. Age categories are intentionally broad and often overlap. They take into account children's interests, content suitability for the age group, and readability. We've used the categories to the left to help guide adults who are choosing from our booklists.

P = PRIMARY (KINDERGARTEN – GRADE 3)
I = INTERMEDIATE (GRADE 3 – GRADE 4)
U = UPPER (GRADE 4 – GRADE 6)

Each title includes a descriptive annotation that captures the heart of the book while outlining specifics such as the age of the character, plot, setting, and historical era. Where appropriate, we've suggested connections: to the world, to history, and to other books on the same theme or topic. The annotations suggest ideas to spark active discussion and extend children's thinking: dramatic plays, writing activities, interviews, artwork, group stories, displays, and music.

We also note where books are part of a series because readers must learn to choose books they like and can read. Reading series books is one step forward for kids. They don't have to get used to new characters, writing style, or settings because they're already familiar with them. Readers of series practice speed and they develop some skills in seeing patterns. Most series readers eventually grow out of a particular series and move on to others—just like adults who like mysteries, romance novels, or books by John Grisham. By introducing one book in a series, adults can then turn children loose in the series, such as Lois Lowry's books about Sam, Arnold Lobel's Frog and Toad tales, and Johanna Hurwitz's stories about everyday kids like Russell and Elisa.

# Five Ways To Stir Up A Buzz Around Books

- **Read aloud in class and at home.** No matter how old, kids love the human voice and the drama of a story well told. You're providing a shared experience among all the listeners, and you're able to stop and pick up on themes and ideas that fit into class and family life.

- **Let children help organize the class or family library** and also recommend books to read. Encouraging kids to say what they think stirs the interest of other children, which multiplies your efforts.

- **Introduce kids to books that have similar themes but are explored differently,** then urge them to talk together about the common threads. It helps them develop critical thinking skills by connecting messages and ideas on their own.

- **Get children to write about what they read**—in journals, response logs, letters to each other, essays—and urge them to relate the messages to their lives. It's no secret that the more you write, the better you read, and the better you read, the more you want to read.

- **Start a class or family book club.** It's a great way to use books as a jumping-off point for shared experiences.

## How To Make the Most of This Book

We hope this book will make it easier for you to navigate the universe of children's literature. Once you or your kids have chosen some good books, the following suggestions will help you and your young reading partners get the most out of your shared experience.

- **Start with any chapter.**

- **Read several books** from one chapter if you're going to lead children to talk about that theme. Discuss each book as its own story first, before moving out to the larger issue or questions. Then read another book on the same theme.

- **Allow time for children to notice.** It's important to note that discussions should roam around in the book you're talking about. Don't merely channel talk toward what the story says about "making a difference" or "how people cope in hard times." Children are prime "noticers" and may need to talk about the pictures, tell about a time when they felt or behaved like the book character, or remind you that they know other books by this author.

- **Clarify what needs further explanation according to kids' knowledge or experience.** Sometimes facts, words, or inferences need clarifying. Take time to talk about those.

- **Reread books.** It is all right to read a book again. Try to keep the first reading as uninterrupted as possible. The second time, pause, notice, and talk about specifics. Young children may want to return to a book again and again and notice different things about it when they do. But older readers frequently reread, too.

- **Look for evidence of children seeing patterns.** Adults may hear statements like, "That's just like the boy in the book we read last week." "There are a lot of 'w' words in this book." "I like 'I' books where the main character tells you her story." "This is just like a folktale, only different." Adults should ask, "Why do you say that?" "How can you tell?" and other open-ended questions. It's important to help children develop the habit of offering evidence for saying why they think what they do when they notice something from a book.

- Look for confirmation that children are **using what they talk about in their lives**—repeating a phrase, making a decision like one of the characters in the book, pointing out another book by the same author. It's proof that kids are piling up their knowledge and organizing it into categories—becoming an "expert" in some small part of literature.

- **Share your enthusiasm** and a love of books as well as laughter and enjoyment over books. It's the single most important thing an adult can do, next to reading aloud to children.

- **Read aloud**, to anyone who'll listen, older or younger. And let readers read to you!

Recently we received a letter from a now-grown child with whom we'd worked in the early 1990s. The young woman was confident that we would understand what she meant when she told us of her recent struggles, but that in spite, or perhaps because, of those struggles, she felt like the character in Mary Hoffman's *Amazing Grace* . . . "When I put my mind to it, I know I can do anything." Though we'd talked together about the book a decade earlier, the memory was still fresh for her.

Books that get kids talking and inspire thinking create lasting memories. Whether you're an educator, librarian, parent, or youth volunteer, talking about books with kids is a rich experience—sometimes eye-opening, sometimes hilarious, often poignant, memorable, and moving. The good news for grownups is that your kids have the potential to be as excited, passionate, and motivated about opening a book as the young people we've described here. They also have the power to be as thoughtful about what they've read. The good news for kids is that reading can be a social treat as well as a solitary activity. Reading a book doesn't have to isolate the reader; reading a book can bring people together.

# Chapter 1

# Living IN A Family

What's the earliest experience you remember with a book? Chances are it was in the context of a family. A cozy cuddle in grandpa's lap, flashlights and giggles under the covers with a brother or sister, a yawning parent reading Margaret Wise Brown's *Goodnight Moon* just one more time before lights out. Like cookies and milk, books and families go together.

Yet today's families may look very different from those of storybooks long ago. Today, a child may live in a family headed by one or two parents, a grandparent, stepparents, or even nonrelatives. Siblings may or may not be biologically related. American children literally come from around the world, either through immigration or adoption. They may not look like other family members or neighbors in their community.

Regardless of how today's families are formed, contemporary children and their families experience many similar joys. They celebrate birthdays, share housework, play games, take vacations, say "cheese" for the camera at weddings and recitals. And when a child makes a bad decision, the consequences and future behavior are usually worked out within the family.

It's also within families that children hear stories about when they were little, learn about the childhood of their relatives, and come to know about their heritage and cultural traditions. At campouts and reunions, on holidays and graduations, families pass these stories on to the next generation. Books reflect the wealth of experiences that families share the world over. In the delicate story, *Grandfather's Journey* by Allen Say, a Japanese boy poignantly shares the duality of the immigrant experience—of living and loving amid two cultures. The bond of family, past and present, secures his place in both worlds. Stories like this provide children with a sense of continuity, connectedness, and stability, even in unstable times.

Along with joys, families deal with many challenges. Children may have to cope with anxiety about a new baby brother or sister, moving to a new neighborhood, worrying about a parent's job or health, or other stresses. Whether or not they've experienced it themselves, most children know another child whose family has been separated by divorce, death, or incarceration. Stories of families working together to overcome bad times—so beautifully demonstrated in books like *A Chair for My Mother* by Vera B. Williams—can nurture resiliency in young readers. This vibrant book tells the story of a child, her waitress mother, and her grandmother saving coins to replace a comfortable armchair destroyed in their apartment fire. In the midst of tragedy, a child comes to appreciate the true comfort a loving family can provide.

## Special Moments

Through reading books, my children and I have become even closer and have shared special moments that we'll all remember forever. Even though my son is now 24 and my daughter 13, we still talk about our favorite books. When my daughter Emily was younger, she loved making up stories after we finished reading for the night. Sometimes they were extensions of the book we'd just read, sometimes just silly stuff. The books we read carried us through an entire range of emotions. When Emily was in the fourth grade, I reached the last chapter of a very moving book and could barely get the words out because I was so emotionally overcome. But that was far from the end of the story. The last page of the book was only a beginning because we passed the book, and our stories about it, along to our friends.

**TERRY WALDRON**
**PARENT/ART TEACHER**
**SPARTA HIGH SCHOOL**
**SPARTA, ILLINOIS**

The books recommended here, although on various topics, have several things in common: they remind readers that others have had similar experiences, that families are connected, and that families are diverse. Whether or not young readers recognize themselves in the characters they meet in these books, they're sure to empathize with some of the dilemmas these characters face.

We hope these books will help children extend their sense of what a family is and cherish their part in it because, as Grace's grandmother says in Mary Hoffman's *Boundless Grace*, "A family with you in it is a real family. Families are what you make them."

**ALLEN SAY** *is an author and illustrator who paints with words and pictures. Say, whose books include **Grandfather's Journey**, is known for his beautifully sensitive style and delicate illustrations.*

***Your family has played a prominent role in many of your books. Why do you think your family's story resonates with readers?***

Every family is on a journey, whether it's the literal journey of recent immigrants or the spiritual journey of families who've been here for generations. I think when people read my books, they see themselves and their own families, no matter what their culture or history. One family's journey is another family's path to discovery.

# RECOMMENDED Books

P = PRIMARY (KINDERGARTEN – GRADE 3)
I = INTERMEDIATE (GRADE 3 – GRADE 4)
U = UPPER (GRADE 4 – GRADE 6)

## Ant Plays Bear

BY BETSY BYARS
ILLUSTRATED BY MARC SIMONT
VIKING, 1997. (I)

In this subtle, loving easy-reader story, Anthony (Ant) plays games of imagination with his older brother. The older brother pretends to be a bear until Ant stops the game because he's a little scared. Then Ant happily pretends to be a dog until a mean-spirited boy suggests that Anthony's brother ditch the "dog." Later, the two brothers agree they'd never do that to a pet. When Ant discusses his feelings about being afraid in the night, his older brother reassures him with patience and ingenuity. The last chapter considers "when Ant grows up" and readers will chuckle at the surprising but apt possibilities, just as Ant's older brother does. Readers can enjoy sharing stories about their adventures with siblings or close friends. They can also talk about the many ways family members show they care for each other.

## Attaboy, Sam!

BY LOIS LOWRY
ILLUSTRATED BY DIANE deGROAT
HOUGHTON MIFFLIN, 1992. (I, U)

This funny novel features a preschooler with a problem: what to give his mother for her birthday? He decides to collect all of her favorite scents into one bottle and let it ripen in his closet. How do families celebrate special events? What makes a celebration memorable? Readers will jump at the opportunity to tell or draw about these times. The humorous "Sam" stories also feature his big sister Anastasia, who has her own books as well. (Series)

## Aunt Flossie's Hats (and Crab Cakes Later)

BY ELIZABETH FITZGERALD HOWARD
ILLUSTRATED BY JAMES E. RANSOME
CLARION, 1991. (P, I)

Using the device of hats to call up memories, a beloved great-great aunt shares her stories with two girls, thus passing along family tales and traditions. Invite readers to talk about treasures—real or remembered. "Treasures" would also make a good labeled classroom or tabletop display or book of writings.

## black is brown is tan

BY ARNOLD ADOFF
ILLUSTRATED BY EMILY ARNOLD McCULLY
AMISTAD, 2002 (1973). (P)

This cheerful, playful word poem celebrates the diversity of the American family, based on the author's own biracial family—a white husband, an African-American wife, two children, and an assortment of grandparents, uncles, and aunts in all sorts of colors, as the title states. Like many families, this one enjoys singing, working, and being together. Older children may be surprised to learn that interracial marriages were illegal in 28 states in 1960, the year in which the author married. Adults may also be interested to know that Adoff's wife was award-winning author Virginia Hamilton, who died in 2002.

## Boundless Grace

BY MARY HOFFMAN
ILLUSTRATED BY CAROLINE BINCH
DIAL, 1995. (P, I)

Grace thinks that Nana and Ma, who is divorced from Grace's father, aren't a real family. "We need a father and a brother and a dog." But when she visits her father and his new family in the Republic of The Gambia, she creates a new definition of family for herself that includes her African family as well as the one she lives with in the city. The thoughtful character Grace was first introduced in Hoffman's *Amazing Grace* (Dial, 1991).

## Brown Angels

BY WALTER DEAN MYERS
HARPERCOLLINS, 1993. (P, I)

Old photographs combine with poems to portray timeless vignettes of children. The author's passion for collecting early photographs, his curiosity about the family stories behind them, and the times in which the subjects lived encourage contemporary readers to look closely at their own era. This book should tempt children to seek out or make up stories about their own old family photographs.

## Bunnicula: A Rabbit Tale of Mystery

BY DEBORAH AND JAMES HOWE
ILLUSTRATED BY LESLIE MORRILL
SIMON & SCHUSTER, 1979. (I, U)

Not only does Harold, the family dog, confront a suspicious bunny with his feline friend Chester, he must deal with sometimes obtuse human behavior. Family life for humans, including sibling rivalry, is pretty funny when examined from Harold's perspective. Taking their cue from Harold, readers can guess at the different ways members of their own families—including the family pet—might view the same incident. (Series)

## A Chair for My Mother

BY VERA B. WILLIAMS
GREENWILLOW, 1983. (P)

A child and her mother and grandmother save coins to buy a comfortable armchair after their belongings are destroyed in an apartment fire. The family works together, the community supports them, and the three parts of the illustrations (frame, major picture, and tiny vignettes) all emphasize what's important in the story. Two other stories about this family (both Greenwillow) are *Something Special for Me* (1983) and *Music, Music for Everyone* (1984).

## Cherry Pies and Lullabies

BY LYNN REISER
GREENWILLOW, 1998. (P, I)

From great-grandmother to child, four generations have four different ways of baking bread, stitching a quilt, or weaving a flower crown. But all generations sing the same lullaby. "Every time it was the same, but different." The book celebrates family traditions handed down from one generation to the next and the importance of traditional women's crafts and activities. *Tortillas and Lullabies/Tortillas Y Cancioncitas* by Lynn Reiser et al. (Greenwillow, 1998) explores similar traditions from Hispanic cultures.

## Dim Sum for Everyone

BY GRACE LIN
KNOPF, 2001. (P)

A family goes out for a special dinner at their favorite *dim sum* restaurant and delights in the "little dishes" that come to the table on a rolling cart. Crisp illustrations using different perspectives show the family's pleasure in the dinner and provide additional information about the Chinese cuisine, *dim sum*. This book could be used to jump start a conversation about family dining traditions as well as foods from different cultures.

## Emma's Yucky Brother

BY JEAN LITTLE
ILLUSTRATED BY JENNIFER PLECAS
HARPERCOLLINS, 2001. (P, I)

Emma is excited when her family adopts four-year-old Max, but he's not nearly as cute or as little as he was in his photographs. Transitions are difficult for everyone as Max moves from foster care into this permanent home, especially for Emma, who is no longer the only child in the family. This short, expressively illustrated chapter book provides a way into many discussable topics such as sibling relationships, adoption, and acceptance.

## Fig Pudding

BY RALPH FLETCHER
CLARION, 1995. (U)

Describing one roller coaster year in the life of a close-knit family with six children, Clifford, the oldest, tells of hilarious times and deeply sad ones, such as the death of his brother. While the brother's death comes as a shock both to the family and to the reader, the many ways the family members remember, grieve, and keep going are a comfort. The emotional impact of the novel makes readers thoughtful about what holds a family together.

## Five Creatures

BY EMILY JENKINS
ILLUSTRATED BY TOMEK BOGACKI
FRANCES FOSTER/FARRAR, STRAUS & GIROUX, 2000. (P)

In a family of three people and two cats, there are many similarities and differences, for instance, four who like to eat fish and two who like to eat mice. The circular pictures emphasize unity and connections. Jenkins provides a strong writing model or conversation starter for comparing patterns within families, clubs, or classrooms.

## Georgie Lee

BY SHARON PHILLIPS DENSLOW
ILLUSTRATED BY LYNNE RAE PERKINS
GREENWILLOW, 2002. (I, U)

This short novel uses understated humor to help readers observe the small things in life and the actions that connect people on a rural farm where J.D. spends the summer with his grandmother and a cow. Tolerance, patience, enjoyment of special moments, and self- and neighborly reliance are some of the values highlighted in this book.

## Gettin' Through Thursday

BY MELROSE COOPER
ILLUSTRATED BY NNEKA BENNETT
LEE & LOW, 1998. (P)

Even though Andre's mother promised a celebration if he achieved honor roll status, he pouts because he has to wait until payday. But the family imaginatively throws him a dress rehearsal party and Andre realizes how much they care about him. Children can talk about times of waiting, promises deferred, or things we think we want or need but can't have.

## Grandaddy and Janetta Together: The Three Stories in One Book

BY HELEN V. GRIFFITH
ILLUSTRATED BY JAMES STEVENSON
GREENWILLOW, 2000. (I)

With understated humor and resonating warmth, this short chapter book combines three picture book stories illustrated with Stevenson's cartoon and watercolor wash. Each story reveals something new about the loving relationship between a Baltimore girl and her grandfather who lives in rural Georgia, both of whom visit each other and provide mutual support in tackling new experiences.

## Grandfather's Journey

BY ALLEN SAY
HOUGHTON MIFFLIN, 1993. (I)

This deceptively simple picture book won awards for its depiction of a life story in which a boy journeys from Japan to California, tours the United States and returns to Japan. There, he lives through a war, and grows old. In telling the story, grandson Say confesses that "the moment I am in one country, I am homesick for the other." Recent immigrants will relate to this feeling but everyone can discuss journeys and homecomings. The family narrative began in *Tree of Cranes* (Houghton Mifflin, 1991) and continues in *Tea with Milk* (Houghton Mifflin, 1999).

## Gus and Grandpa and Show-and-Tell

BY CLAUDIA MILLS
ILLUSTRATED BY CATHERINE STOCK
FARRAR, STRAUS & GIROUX, 2000. (I)

Struggling over what to bring to his second grade show-and-tell, Gus decides to bring in Grandpa, who can tell tales of his parents' settling in

Colorado. In other books in this easy-reader series, the two have dealt with Grandpa's forgetful nature, a trip to the hospital, cleaning the shed, Gus's desire to ride a two-wheeler, and various holiday dilemmas. Not only do Gus and Grandpa think through problems, they also consider different options before settling on the best one—a good model for working through a snag or difficulty. (Series)

## Henry and Mudge in the Family Trees

BY CYNTHIA RYLANT
ILLUSTRATED BY SUÇIE STEVENSON
SIMON & SCHUSTER, 1997. (I)

Henry's nervousness about attending a family reunion disappears when he has a full day of food and fun. Best of all, his big dog Mudge is the hit of the party. This is one of many books in an easy-reader series that explores family situations with warmth while imparting gentle messages. (Series)

## Henry's First Moon Birthday

BY LENORE LOOK
ILLUSTRATED BY YUMI HEO
ATHENEUM, 2001. (P)

Jen helps her Chinese-American family prepare for the traditional one-month birthday celebration for baby Henry. Not only does the author convey information about this cultural celebration, she invites listeners to compare ways other families mark important days. Along these same lines, Pam Muñoz Ryan's funny *Mice and Beans* (illustrated by Joe Cepeda, Scholastic, 2001) shows a typical Mexican-American birthday celebration, which is at first hampered and then saved by pesky mice.

## How Tiá Lola Came to Visit/Stay

BY JULIA ALVAREZ
KNOPF, 2001. (U)

When Tiá Lola moves from the Dominican Republic to Vermont to help out, Miguel is mortified by her flamboyant character and her willingness to make friends with anyone. He's still smarting from his parents' divorce, disoriented by his own subsequent move, and terribly worried that he won't fit in with his new neighbors. The author invites readers to talk about new situations and how families come through them.

## If You Ever Get Lost

BY BARBARA ANN PORTE
ILLUSTRATED BY NANCY CARPENTER
GREENWILLOW, 1999. (I)

A chapter book filled with small domestic incidents that read as if a child were saying, "One time in my family, we … " In one instance, the children become separated from their mother while watching their father run a race, but with a little ingenuity they figure out how to find her. In another scene, Mother is annoyed at the children for loading dog bowls, leashes, toys, and other items into a shopping cart for the dog the family hopes they'll get. But the contents of the cart turn out to be just the thing another desperate shopper needs. One rainy day, the children bake brownies, then try to divide them evenly and play imaginatively indoors with their new umbrellas. Nine short chapters are perfect for reading aloud and talking about how children solve small problems like what to do on a rainy day or how to behave when something unexpected happens.

## In My Family/En Mi Familia

BY CARMEN LOMAS GARZA
CHILDREN'S BOOK PRESS, 1996. (I, U)

From watching horned toads and getting haircuts to preparing cactus for dinner and playing games, the author captures her Mexican-American childhood in Texas with visual and textual details that encourage children to draw and talk about their own traditions and celebrations. In Spanish and English.

## Just One More Story

BY JENNIFER BRUTSCHY
ILLUSTRATED BY CAT BOWMAN SMITH
ORCHARD, 2002. (P)

Austin travels in a small trailer with his musician parents, and each night he hears one story. But he always asks for one more. He gets another story when the family stays in a "two-story house." Back on the road again, it's one story per night until they decide to treat themselves to a hotel—with 11 stories. The illustrations cleverly keep track of the stories Dad tells by arraying them in the space above his head. Young readers will have fun identifying the story-circles, which provide a good inventory of stories no child should leave kindergarten without hearing.

## Love, Ruby Lavender

BY DEBORAH WILES
GULLIVER BOOKS, 2001. (U)

Ruby and her grandmother, Eula Garnet, share everything in their small Mississippi town, from rescuing captive chickens to mourning the death of Grandpa Garnet. When Eula decides to visit Hawaii, Ruby fills her days writing letters and coping with her nemesis, Melba, whose dislike for Ruby seems to be linked to some secret about Grandpa Garnet. Loss, family secrets, and making amends are handled with humor and sensitivity in this warmly written novel.

## My Rotten Redheaded Older Brother

BY PATRICIA POLACCO
SIMON & SCHUSTER, 1994. (I)

Patricia has a teasing, challenging, and gross older brother who is her constant torment. However, his behavior when she falls off a merry-go-round proves something important to her and to readers about how people show they care for each other. Because Polacco has written so many excellent picture books about her family history, she would make a fine author/illustrator study for second and third graders.

## The Night Worker

BY KATE BANKS
ILLUSTRATED BY GEORG HALLENSLEBEN
FRANCIS FOSTER BOOKS/FARRAR, STRAUS & GIROUX, 2000. (P)

Usually Alex's dad kisses him and then goes off to work, but this evening Alex gets his own hard hat and enters the world of the construction worker. Father and son share the excitement of the city at night and the wonders of machines onsite. Illustrations use dark line and earth tones to enhance the wonder of the night. Fathers and their children will enjoy sharing other books, such as *Owl Moon* by Jane Yolen, (illustrated by John Schoenherr, Philomel, 1987) or *How Many Stars in the Sky* by Lenny Hort (illustrated by James E. Ransome, Morrow, 1991), in which a boy and his dad try to count stars on a warm summer night.

## Our Only May Amelia

BY JENNIFER L. HOLM
HarperCollins, 1999. (U)

As the only girl in a family of seven boys in the late 1800s in Washington state, May Amelia has adventures her father considers unladylike, deals with an unpleasant and angry grandmother, and wishes for a sister. Her strong character shows how someone develops strength, values, and independent spirit within a large family. The story was inspired by the author's discovery of the diary of her grandmother, the real May Amelia.

## Owen

BY KEVIN HENKES
GREENWILLOW, 1993. (P)

Owen, a young mouse, loves his yellow blanket, Fuzzy, but he's getting a bit big to carry it everywhere. Owen and his parents, with some not-too-useful advice from nosey neighbor Mrs. Tweezers, come up with a clever and workable solution. The way in which Owen and his parents solve this problem inspires children to talk about objects that were important to them when they were little.

## Owen Foote, Money Man

BY STEPHANIE GREENE
ILLUSTRATED BY MARTHA WESTON
CLARION, 2000. (I)

Owen's crazy money-making schemes don't work. But when he decides to be a fishpond "consultant" to his elderly neighbor, Owen learns that it's the teamwork, respect, and companionship he values, not the surprising money he earns. Believable dialogue, a contemporary family with a cheerfully disdainful older sister, and typical family incidents add strength to this short chapter book. (Series)

## Pete's a Pizza

BY WILLIAM STEIG
HarperCollins, 1998. (P)

Pete's in a bad mood, a grumpy black hole, so his parents playfully make Pete into a pizza. It's not long before Pete is stifling giggles as he's sprinkled with tomatoes that are really checkers and carried to the sofa to "bake." This is a fine story for talking about ways to turn a bad day around and how others in the family and a good sense of humor can help.

### The Relatives Came
BY CYNTHIA RYLANT
ILLUSTRATED BY STEPHEN GAMMELL
BRADBURY PRESS, 1985. (P, I)

The annual Ohio visit from the Virginia relatives
is full of welcome hugs, sharing floor space,
fixing up the place, and eating. And then, two
weeks later, it's time for goodbye hugs. Readers
can talk about the joys and the challenges of
this family's visits as a precursor to discussing
or writing about their own.

### Saffy's Angel
BY HILARY MCKAY
MARGARET MCELDERRY BOOKS/SIMON & SCHUSTER, 2002. (U)

Artists Eve and Bill Casson have named each
of their children after a color—Rose, Indigo,
Cadmium, and Saffron. When Saffy learns she's
adopted, her quest for her heritage leads her to
Italy and a fiercely independent friend, Sarah—a
"wheelchair kid." There she discovers the details
of her adoption by her mother's twin sister after
a car crash. Humor and unforgettably eccentric
characters in a fast-paced plot will trigger talk of
loss, adoption, and what creates a family and
its history.

### Same Stuff as Stars
BY KATHERINE PATERSON
CLARION, 2002. (U)

When their self-absorbed mother takes 11-year-
old Angel and her younger brother to live with
their great-grandmother on her dilapidated
Vermont farm, Angel's adult concerns are assuaged
by a mysterious, stargazing stranger. He turns
out to be her uncle, a Vietnam veteran with a
difficult past. This touching story explores how
families and individuals change, what forgiveness
is, and how families cope during tough times.

### Seven Brave Women
BY BETSY HEARNE
ILLUSTRATED BY BETHANNE ANDERSEN
GREENWILLOW, 1997. (I)

Looking back through generations, a girl tells a bit
about each of seven female relatives who quietly
shaped history as they went about their lives in
difficult times of war. Each relative has endowed
this modern-day narrator with a trait, talent, or
affinity. Talking about this book will give readers a
chance to consider the many ways that family
traits can be handed down, regardless of whether
the ties are those of blood or affection.

### Shirley's Wonderful Baby
BY VALISKA GREGORY
ILLUSTRATED BY BRUCE DEGEN
HARPERCOLLINS, 2002. (P)

Shirley jealously counts the ways everyone is
wrong when they think her new brother is
"wonderful." But when Mrs. Mump, the babysitter,
pays full attention to Shirley and suggests that
she will have to handle the feeding and diapering,
Shirley discovers that she just may like the baby
after all. This is a classic sibling rivalry theme,
echoed in many other books, such as Henkes'
*Julius, the Baby of the World* (Greenwillow, 1999)
and Jane Cutler's *Darcy and Gran Don't Like Babies*
(Scholastic, 1993).

### Shortcut
BY DONALD CREWS
GREENWILLOW, 1992. (P, I)

While visiting their grandparents in the rural
south, the narrator and his cousins take a forbidden shortcut home along railroad tracks. They
narrowly avert disaster as a freight train forces
them to jump from the tracks into unseen dangers
below. The children arrive home safely, though
frightened and wiser, and vow never to tell the
adults what happened. Readers can explore why
the children didn't tell and whether they should
have. Crews introduces the setting of his childhood summers in *Bigmama's* (Greenwillow, 1991).
Crews usually incorporates numerals for the year
in which he finished the book in one of his illustrations, typically one year before the publication
date. Look closely for "91."

### Song of the Trees
BY MILDRED TAYLOR
ILLUSTRATED BY JERRY PINKNEY
DIAL, 1975. (I)

During the Great Depression of the 1920s and 30s,
it was rare for African Americans to own land and
farm it, but the Logan family is exceptional in
doing both. When Cassie Logan's father is forced
to leave their Mississippi farm to earn enough for
taxes, an unscrupulous white man tries to cheat
the family out of the old-growth trees on their
property. This short novel introduces a historical

period, the need for civil rights that would not come for several decades, and a strong family whose stories are continued in successively lengthier novels. Older readers will be riveted by the Newbery Medal-winning *Roll of Thunder, Hear My Cry* (Dial, 1975) and *The Land* (Dial, 2001).

## The Storytellers

BY TED LEWIN
LOTHROP, LEE & SHEPARD, 1998. (P)

Abdul and his grandfather walk to work through the old *medina* or marketplace passing by dye stalls, copper and brass workers, date sellers, and other vendors, to spread a rug by the Moroccan city gate. Slowly people gather, a pet pigeon soars into the air to bring back a story, and Grandfather begins to speak. Gazing at pictures packed with information, readers can discuss why the time-honored occupation of storytelling is so important. Older children may recognize the story-telling conventions Grandfather uses here. Over half of the book is devoted to a fascinating tour of the *medina*. Note how Lewin's watercolors depicting a Moroccan dye market are validated by a similar view in an aerial photograph in *Earth from Above for Young Readers*, discussed in Chapter 5.

## The Stray Dog

BY MARC SIMONT
HARPERCOLLINS, 2001. (P)

Away from the city where they live, a family goes on a picnic in a park. There, the two children enjoy playing with a collarless and seemingly homeless dog they call Willy and wish they could take home. But the mother points out that his owners would miss him. When they return to the park again the next week, the lonely dog is still there, but the dogcatcher looms. Luckily, the children think of a clever way to trick the dog-catcher and persuade their parents to adopt Willy. Simont's eloquent illustrations show deep emotion with simplicity and cleverly note the passage of time as the distracted family members worry about Willy for the week. The story will prompt readers to talk about how they got their own pets or discuss what they would do with a pet if they had one.

## Tell Me A Story, Mama

BY ANGELA JOHNSON
ILLUSTRATED BY DAVID SOMAN
ORCHARD BOOKS, 1989. (P)

A girl asks her mother to tell a story about when Mama was little and then proceeds to tell it herself. The child's familiarity with the story provides an entrée into a discussion of how snippets of family history fit together to give a person a sense of place in the world. This intimate technique of a dialogue between child and adult about times past was also used by Marie-Louise Fitzpatrick in *You, Me and the Big Blue Sea* (Roaring Brook Press, 2002).

## Toasting Marshmallows: Camping Poems

BY KRISTINE O'CONNELL
ILLUSTRATED BY KATE KIESLER
CLARION, 2000. (I, U)

Told from a child's point of view, these inviting poems chronicle a family camping trip and communicate feelings, observations, and reflection with humor and thoughtfulness. Children will identify with the challenges of being someplace new and the thoughts travel evokes.

## Trolls

BY POLLY HORVATH
FARRAR, STRAUS & GIROUX, 1999. (U)

Melissa, Amanda, and Frank (*aka* Peewee) meet their babysitter, Aunt Sally, for the first time when their parents leave for Paris. Aunt Sally is full of surprises, but she teaches the children the importance of family connectedness and warns of letting trolls, an intriguing metaphor for what happens when families don't communicate, infiltrate one's life. Quirky characters use humor to explore what could be difficult topics. The author's Newbery honor book, *Everything on a Waffle* (Farrar, Straus & Giroux, 2001), also celebrates an unusual family and the strength that comes of hanging on to your beliefs in difficult times.

## 26 Fairmont Street

BY TOMIE DE PAOLA
PUTNAM, 1999. (P, I)

The humorous, memorable, memoirs of this well-known picture book author/artist began with this Newbery Honor book. In it, five-year-old Tomie recalls his first day of kindergarten, the Disney film

*Snow White*, and of course, his relatives. This warm humorous look at one family is sure to inspire a reader's own remembrances. These short, generously illustrated biographies also reintroduce de Paola to seven- and eight-year-olds, who probably first met him when they were three or four. Those familiar with his Irish or Italian folktales, Strega Nona stories, or his many informational and picture books, can see where de Paola gets his ideas. (Series)

## Uncle Elephant
BY ARNOLD LOBEL
HarperCollins, 1981. (P)

When his parents are lost at sea, the narrator is left alone, but only until old Uncle Elephant arrives. The young elephant learns and laughs with his wrinkly uncle while he longs for his parents who finally, and reassuringly, return. This winning easy-reader story told in nine very short chapters, provides children with a chance to talk about how people cheer each other up in distressing times and an invitation to recount stories about their favorite relatives or caregivers.

## The Watsons Go to Birmingham—1963
BY CHRISTOPHER PAUL CURTIS
Delacorte Press, 1995. (U)

Kenny's older brother Byron is a handful—setting fires, getting an unauthorized "conk" hairdo, and freezing his lips to the car's rearview mirror. His parents decide to take him to his no-nonsense Grandma in Alabama where they inadvertently witness one of the most horrible moments in the Civil Rights era, a church bombing that killed four girls. By turns heartbreaking and hilarious, this book introduces an important time in history and shows how individuals in a family help each other cope with challenges.

## We Wanted You
BY LIZ ROSENBERG
Illustrated by Peter Catalanotto
Roaring Brook Press, 2002. (P, I)

As Enrique stands in cap and gown at his high school graduation, his parents narrate the story of how they prepared for his adoption many years earlier. The spare, poetic text is accompanied by watercolors that show how Enrique grew from a baby who was welcomed by a loving family into a confident and proud young adult. This poignant story will generate talk about how adoption creates families and why parents and children sometimes don't look alike. Children will also note the way the illustrations depict Enrique's growth. Another fine book about adoption, Jean Okimoto and Elaine Aoki's *The White Swan Express* (illustrated by Meilo So, Clarion, 2002), presents four diverse sets of parents who befriend each other while adopting Chinese daughters.

## Yang the Youngest and His Terrible Ear
BY LENSEY NAMIOKA
Illustrated by Kees de Kiefte
Little Brown, 1992. (I, U)

Yang is adrift in his musically inclined family because he's tone deaf and immune to the violin's charms. A recent immigrant to the United States, Yang wants to play baseball. Yang's new friend is a good violinist and an indifferent ball player, so the two decide to switch places at a recital and a game. Both sets of parents get to see their boys in a new light and relax their demands. The story invites readers to talk about the dilemmas and power of parental expectations. Four other novels chronicle the lives of this Chinese-American family, each from the point of view of a different sibling. (Series)

## Zack in the Middle
BY DIA L. MICHAELS
Illustrated by Fred Bell
Platypus Media, 2001. (I)

Being the middle kid is never easy and it's even worse when you're the only boy with a too-busy older sister and an adorable younger sister. But being part of a loving family can make up for the downside of being stuck in the middle. Children should have fun arguing the relative merits of being the middle child (or younger or older child for that matter) and thinking about whether they would want to trade places with someone else in their family.

# Bath, Book, and
# Beyond

My kids were "bouncing off the walls" at bedtime, and even though I'm a child development specialist, the kids were winning the battle. When I called on my training, I realized what was missing—a routine. So, I established a bedtime routine around reading. The first sequence, (1) bath, (2) book, (3) song, (4) bedtime, quickly became (1) bath, (2) book after book after book after book. Reading books at bedtime is such a great way for us to subtly talk through the day's experiences. I still read to my kids every day, including my 13-year-old, who of course could read the books herself. But reading aloud involves all three children, and they each get something out of it on their own level. My kids are enthralled with reading—they're in the car right now, waiting for me to drive them to the library.

**BETSY DARDEN-JONES**
**PARENT OF A 13-, 7-, AND 6-YEAR-OLD**

## Chapter 2

# Going TO School

The snap of a new three-ring binder. The feel of fresh blue-lined paper. The sight of perfectly pointed tips in a brand new box of crayons. What excitement—and terror—the first day of school can bring! Whether it's a kindergartner dragging her first book bag, a middle-schooler changing classrooms for the first time, or the new kid in class who speaks a different language, students find in books the familiar friends they need to help them on their way.

School is the place where children master curriculum, make friends, and learn to navigate unfamiliar territory. Next to families, school is the second most important developmental influence children have. As they come to remember which desk is theirs, experiment with different foods in the cafeteria, and practice civilized classroom decorum, new students also learn all sorts of important things about themselves as people. Still, while school is a wonderful and exciting challenge, it has its rough spots.

The books in this section explore the array of experiences children have in school. Some of these books tell stories about new experiences and new people. Others touch on issues such as talking to teachers about a problem, being "good" in a subject, learning English as a second language, understanding math, producing art, conquering a subject area, or simply making it through the school day. From the bittersweet *My Name is Jorge: On Both Sides of the River* by Jane Medina to the wonderfully irreverent *Math Curse* by Jon Scieszka and Lane Smith, these books explore situations children will readily recognize.

This chapter also presents stories about children in school settings outside of mainstream North American culture. These stories remind readers that education isn't a universally held privilege; some children work very hard to be allowed to attend school. By the same token, young readers will be fascinated that children in classrooms across the globe share similar experiences and challenges.

Many titles here consider the emotions school evokes: fear of speaking or performing in front of an audience, shyness, embarrassment, joy at learning to sing or play an instrument, loneliness before finding a friend and a place in school. In fact, nearly all of the books in this chapter emphasize the importance that friendship plays in making a child feel good in school. This matter of making friends is such a deep, rich, and significant one, both in children's lives and in children's literature, that it has its own chapter in this book.

## Can I Have Another One?

It's time to change the perception that book clubs are for adult intellectuals. As a matter of fact, fourth- and fifth-grade members are just as insightful. I've found that once the word spreads about a good book or a lively meeting, more kids want to join. Even reluctant students become enthusiastic over exciting books! Judy Blume's *Fudge* series is among my students' favorites. My students constantly stop me in the hallway to tell me, "I'm on chapter six!" or "I'm finished with this book—can I have another one?"

TERI NIELSEN
READING TEACHER
DEALE ELEMENTARY SCHOOL
CHESAPEAKE, MARYLAND

As children learn, they can slide into a certain complacency. They might peg themselves as being only interested in math, or no good in art, or a great reader, or someone who hates poetry. Part of the magic of teaching is tempting students to venture outside their own personal stereotypes. In so doing, teachers often find themselves bucking parallel stereotypes in society. How many times have you heard the myths that "only boys like nonfiction" or "only girls like poetry"? Inspired teachers know that everyone is fascinated with nature's workings, famous people, or the qualities of water. Likewise, they know, just like in *Love That Dog* by Sharon Creech, that boys can respond powerfully to rhythm, rhyme, form, and the content of poetry.

Child readers probably won't focus on the teaching and teachers in these stories, concentrated as they are on the child at the center of the book. But adults will be sympathetic to, and perhaps encouraged by, the many fine teachers represented in the children's books selected here. The exuberant Mr. Slinger, the sensitive Mr. Falker, the tenacious and creative Miss Agnes, and the ever-tolerant Mrs. Pigeon are passionate, patient, and caring educators whose example make this profession a proud and beautiful one.

**PATRICIA POLACCO** *is a prolific writer whose story of her own childhood struggle with dyslexia became the subject of her popular book,* **Thank You, Mr. Falker***. In this book, Polacco's poignant tale of painful teasing by classmates and the intervention of one special teacher gave children the world over a story of hope.*

### Why is *Thank You, Mr. Falker* so important to your readers?

This book helps children see that even successful adults haven't always had it easy. Many of my readers weren't aware I had a learning disability. I want kids to know that no matter what struggles they face, they really can overcome them, especially with the help of a kind and caring teacher. I believe in a teacher's power to improve a child's life by discovering the source of that child's pain and helping the child believe in herself. Mr. Falker did that for me by discovering my reading problem and getting me the help I needed. He also helped me realize I was a gifted artist. Schools and classrooms truly are places where magic can happen.

# RECOMMENDED Books

P = PRIMARY (KINDERGARTEN – GRADE 3)
I = INTERMEDIATE (GRADE 3 – GRADE 4)
U = UPPER (GRADE 4 – GRADE 6)

## Brave as a Mountain Lion

BY ANN HERBERT SCOTT
ILLUSTRATED BY GLO COALSON
CLARION, 1996. (P, I)

When Spider is invited to participate in his school spelling bee, he's terrified until each member of his Shoshone family offers him advice. Spider uses this advice to find his own courage in a book that presents both the distinctiveness of Shoshone life in modern day Nevada and the universality of stage fright.

## Class President

BY JOHANNA HURWITZ
MORROW, 1990. (U)

Julio decides to help his best friend run for fifth-grade class president, but as incidents arise, it's obvious that Julio is the one who would make a good leader. Readers may notice how Julio develops responsibility, mediation and negotiating abilities, and tact in contrast to his opinionated opponent Cricket Kaufman. This is a great book for discussing problem-solving skills. Readers were introduced to this group of friends in *Class Clown* (Morrow, 1987).

## Crow Boy

BY TARO YASHIMA
VIKING, 1955. (P, I)

Over half a century after its original publication date, this Japanese story of classmates' unkind treatment of a silent boy with special abilities is still powerful. It takes a compassionate teacher to discover and help Chibi reveal the unique talents he possesses—talents that make his classmates regret their own hasty judgments. Children like to talk about why the artist painted a butterfly and a flower blooming on the endpapers—a captivating example of visual symbolism.

## David's Drawings

BY CATHRYN FALWELL
LEE & LOW, 2001. (P)

Shy David wins his classmates' attention when he sketches a wintry leafless tree he's seen on his way to school. Nine classmates offer suggestions to "make it even better" and some even help with the additions, such as adding green grass, birds, stickers, and a ballerina self-portrait. Then, the wintry picture becomes springy, a subtle metaphor of David's blooming with all of this attention. After recess spent playing with his new friends, he places the group picture on the classroom wall and labels it "Our Class Picture." But he also realizes his original intentions when he draws this scene at home and titles it "My Drawing," allowing the author to convey the message that it's fun to create art together and it's fine to have your own artistic vision, too. Falwell's bright fabric and cut-paper collages invite readers to make their own seasonal pictures in the same collage medium, either in collaboration or happily alone.

## Dear Whiskers

BY ANN WHITEHEAD NAGDA
ILLUSTRATED BY STEPHANIE ROTH
HOLIDAY HOUSE, 2000. (I)

Fourth grader Jenny's class assignment is to write to a second-grade pen pal as if she (Jenny) were a mouse. Inexplicably, Sameera won't write back. When Jenny discovers why—that Sameera is newly arrived from Saudi Arabia and can't speak English—she launches a plan to help. This book might spark an across-grade pen pal project and certainly will spark interest in the challenges of learning about a new culture, from the perspective of both native and newcomer.

## Elizabeti's School

BY STEPHANIE STUVE-BODEEN
ILLUSTRATED BY CHRISTY HALE
LEE & LOW, 2002. (P, I)

Engaging Elizabeti, a young Tanzanian girl, wishes she were home with her mother until she realizes she's learned things at school she can show off to her family. As in *Where Are You Going, Manyoni?* by Catherine Stock (Morrow, 1993), this picture book can be read as information about what schools look like in parts of Africa or as a story of the difficulties and rewards of getting to and being in school. Both books invite readers to think about schools in other countries and value the lives of the people who live there. This is the third book about Elizabeti.

## First Graders from Mars: Horus's Horrible Day

BY SHANA COREY
ILLUSTRATED BY MARK TEAGUE
SCHOLASTIC, 2001. (P)

Now that he's in first grade, Horus longs for the old days in Martiangarten, though things start to look up when he meets a new girl from Phobos. Teague's loopy depiction of the various Martian children—who are antenna-ed, multi-limbed, and colorful—begs readers to draw their own versions of these extraterrestrials. By removing the first day of school from the human realm and putting it in an alien setting, this book takes a humorous look at first-day jitters, inviting readers to share other stories of dealing with new experiences and to talk about how parents, teachers, and friends can help. (Series)

## Flying Solo

BY RALPH FLETCHER
CLARION, 1998. (U)

When Mr. Fabiano calls in sick and the substitute teacher fails to show up, the sixth-grade class takes over. Suspense builds as readers wonder if the class can pull it off: Will anarchy reign? Will the usual personal animosities surface? Amazingly, the students manage to hide their lack of a teacher, conduct the business of the day, and discuss a host of emotional issues and ethical questions. Only at the end does the principal discover what's going on. The story invites older readers to talk about what makes a classroom a good learning place, how students treat substitute teachers, the role of individual responsibility with or without an adult present, and whether the principal's treatment of the class was just.

## Frindle

BY ANDREW CLEMENT
ILLUSTRATED BY BRIAN SELZNICK
SIMON & SCHUSTER, 1996. (U)

Ten-year-old Nick coins a new word for "pen" to test the way words get added to the English language—or to waste valuable class time fooling around, according to his teacher, Mrs. Granger. The word catches on and Nick unleashes events that begin to spin out of control. The story, which comes full circle, gives readers a glimpse of the adult Nick becomes and may spark discussion of the bumpiness of growing up. Like Clement's *The Landry News* (Simon & Schuster, 1999), the book portrays life in the classroom in which both children and teachers mature and change.

## Hooway for Wodney Wat

BY HELEN LESTER
ILLUSTRATED BY LYNN MUNSINGER
WALTER LORRAINE, 1999. (P)

Big, mean, smart Camilla Capybara torments shy Wodney Wat and his classmates, but Wodney learns that his classmates like him for who he is when he directs the class during a game of Simon Says. Says Wodney, "Go west," and only Camilla doesn't get it, but it's a trick she richly deserves. Readers see that it's an individual's character, not his or her shyness, speech impediment, or other problem, that matters most.

## If You're Not Here, Please Raise Your Hand: Poems About School

BY KALLI DAKOS
ILLUSTRATED BY G. BRIAN KARAS
MACMILLAN, 1990. (I, U)

Humorous and thoughtful poems present in short bits many of the emotions children experience in the course of a school day. Class periods, distractions, a yawning teacher, lining up, hiding in the bathroom, name-calling, and substitute teachers—each poem evokes some familiar topic in a new way. See other collections of Dakos' rhymes in *The Bug in Teacher's Coffee* (HarperCollins, 1999) and *Put Your Eyes Up Here* (Simon & Schuster, 2003).

## Jamaica and the Substitute Teacher

BY JUANITA HAVILL
ILLUSTRATED BY ANNE SIBLEY O'BRIEN
HOUGHTON MIFFLIN, 1999. (P)

Jamaica excels in math and reading and gladly shows off for the substitute teacher. But during a tough spelling test, Jamaica cheats to impress her teacher. When she guiltily confesses, Jamaica earns the respect of the teacher who tells her, "You don't have to be perfect to be special in my class." This fourth story about Jamaica presents classroom pressures, temptations, and ethical dilemmas in ways young children can understand. (Series)

## King of the Kooties

BY DEBBIE DADEY
ILLUSTRATED BY KEVIN O'MALLEY
WALKER, 1999. (I)

This easy chapter book maintains a light tone while dealing with a common topic—bullies. Two fourth-grade friends are targeted by the class bully, Louisa, who calls one of them Kootie King. The boys retaliate in several ways, but by making Louisa princess of their imaginary Kootie Kingdom, they show how humor can sometimes overcome mean-spirited behavior.

## Lilly's Purple Plastic Purse

BY KEVIN HENKES
GREENWILLOW, 1996. (P)

Lilly loves everything about school, especially Mr. Slinger, her teacher. Still, after being reprimanded, she loses her temper and angrily writes him a nasty note. The exuberant pictures invite readers to talk about classroom life and to notice the many visual clues to Lilly's changing feelings. But the real theme is behaving appropriately in school and what to do when you've blown it. Other stories featuring the irrepressible Lilly include *Chester's Way* (Greenwillow, 1988) and *Julius, the Baby of the World* (Greenwillow, 1991).

## Love That Dog

BY SHARON CREECH
HARPERCOLLINS, 2000. (I, U)

With the patient help of his third-grade teacher, Miss Stretchberry, Jack gradually changes his mind about poetry, what it does, and how it works. He also uses poetry to come to grips with his feelings about his dog's death the previous year. Told in journal entries, the story engages readers with multiple ideas, including how school provides time for growth, how teachers help, and how sharing grief helps us deal with it.

## Marianthe's Story: Painted Words/Spoken Memories

BY ALIKI
GREENWILLOW, 1998. (P, I, U)

Woven through this clever book are two stories: Marianthe's version of her family's life before and as they journeyed to America and her experiences in Mr. Petrie's classroom as she is gradually able to tell her story, not only in pictures, but in her new language of English. Based on the author's own experiences, this book invites readers to talk about the political turmoil that propelled the family to come to America and encourages them to consider ways Marianthe's teacher and classmates support her. Interestingly, Aliki based Mr. Petrie, the teacher in this book, in part on the wonderful Mr. Slinger in Kevin Henkes' *Lilly's Purple Plastic Purse*.

## Marvin One Too Many

BY KATHERINE PATERSON
ILLUSTRATED BY JANE CLARK BROWN
HARPERCOLLINS, 2001. (P, I)

Marvin feels out of place and unwelcome in first grade until, with the support of his family, he slowly learns to read. Both for those who are struggling to learn and those who have already learned, this book will surely prompt children to talk about what was hard about beginning to read, what techniques and which people helped, and what they think they still have to learn. (Series)

## Math Curve

BY JON SCIESZKA AND LANE SMITH
VIKING, 1995. (U)

In one great romp through mathematics, a child sees her whole day in terms of math problems, some solvable and some ludicrous. This book invites older children to see math in everyday life, but it also begins a discussion of what's tricky about math for some people. Note that the jacket copy, front matter, Mrs. Fibonacci's name, and the dedication are math-related, as well.

## Molly's Pilgrim

BY BARBARA COHEN
ILLUSTRATED BY MICHAEL DERANEY
LOTHROP, 1983. (I, U)

New to this country, Molly misunderstands who Pilgrims are and makes a model of her immigrant mother instead of a historical figure. But with the help of her teacher, Molly shows the other students the metaphorical, or true, meaning of Thanksgiving. A classic story, this book has endured because of its power to evoke discussion of how and why people immigrate and what they might have to be thankful for. The book was newly illustrated by Daniel Duffy in 1998.

## My Name is Jorge: On Both Sides of the River

BY JANE MEDINA
ILLUSTRATED BY FABRICIO VANDEN BROEK
BOYDS MILLS, 1999. (I, U)

With bittersweet and sometimes moving poems (in both Spanish and English), Jorge tells of his days in school, making friends, and the many small moments when he feels either accepted or rejected. The poems, chronologically arranged as a story, show a Mexican-American child successfully, but not entirely painlessly, blending his experiences in a new school with his family life. Juan Felipe Herrera tells a similar story from his childhood for younger readers in *The Upside Down Boy/El Niño de Cabeza*, vibrantly illustrated by Elizabeth Gomez (Children's Book Press, 2000).

## The Name Jar

BY YANGSOOK CHOI
KNOPF, 2001. (P, I)

After moving from Korea, Unhei is unsure whether to keep her old name and doesn't know what new name to pick. Her classmates place suggestions in a jar until Joey steals it to encourage Unhei to keep her old name, which she does. Be sure to read the jacket note in which the author says she adopted "Rachel" as her American name and now goes by both to give credence to both sides of the debate over choosing an American name versus using your name from your own culture.

## Owen Foote, Second Grade Strongman

BY STEPHANIE GREENE
ILLUSTRATED BY DEE DEROSA
CLARION, 1996. (I)

As the smallest person in his class, Owen is sensitive to the school nurse calling him a "pipsqueak" and pointing out his best friend's greater weight. So Owen speaks up and finds himself in trouble until he and the nurse talk it out. Children can appreciate the diversity of sizes and shapes present in one classroom, but the larger messages are those of accepting what you can't change and working on the things you want to change.

## The Recess Queen

BY ALEXIS O'NEILL
ILLUSTRATED BY LAURA HULISKA-BEIGH
SCHOLASTIC, 2002. (P)

No one dares to do anything until Mean Jean says they can or she will "hammer 'em, slammer 'em, kitz and kajammer 'em." But when a new girl, Katie Sue, joins the class and invites Jean to jump rope with her, Jean's playground bullying days come to an end. Exuberant word play invites readers to chime in with playground chants of their own, and the underlying drama should get students talking about whether or not it's all that easy to diffuse bullying with friendship.

## The Royal Bee

BY FRANCES PARK AND GINGER PAK
ILLUSTRATED BY CHRISTOPHER ZHONG-YUAN ZHANG
BOYDS MILLS, 1999. (P, I)

Song-ho overcomes poverty in his 19th-century Korean village by tenaciously seeking an education. Based on recollections of the authors' grandfather, this story can be used with Elizabeth Fitzgerald Howard's *Virgie Goes to School with Us Boys* (Simon & Schuster, 1999) to talk about why people wish to go to school and what kind of behaviors help someone succeed in life.

## Ruby's Wish

BY SHIRIN YIM BRIDGES
ILLUSTRATED BY SOPHIE BLACKALL
CHRONICLE, 2002. (I)

In a time in China when few girls were taught to read, Ruby longs to go to the university. Her grandfather, with over a hundred grandchildren, sympathetically takes an interest and she becomes one of the very first female students at the university. This is based on a true story from the author's family. Other fictional sketches of hard-earned education inspired by the lives of real people include Booker T. Washington's story told in *More Than Anything Else* by Marie Bradby, illustrated by Chris Soentpiet (Orchard, 1993), and *Richard Wright and the Library Card* by William Miller, illustrated by Gregory Christie (Lee & Low, 1997).

## Running the Road to ABC

BY DENIZE LAUTURE
ILLUSTRATED BY REYNOLD RUFFINS
SIMON & SCHUSTER, 1996. (P, I)

Boys and girls, all schoolchildren, embark on a lush, tropical journey from their home in rural Haiti to their small schoolhouse. Readers can discuss why the children are so anxious to start on the road to ABC and why they scramble so happily to get to school. The author's poetic use of language and imagery might inspire children to write about their own journeys to and from school.

## The Secret School

BY AVI
HARCOURT, 2001. (U)

Sharp dialogue, interesting characters, and a 1925 Colorado setting help tell the story of 14-year-old Ida, who takes over the daunting task of teaching in her one-room schoolhouse to prevent its closure for lack of an instructor. Ida needs a diploma to go on to high school and to become a certified teacher herself. This quiet "survival" story evokes talk about school in another era, the value of an education, and how a strong character works to get what she needs.

## 7 X 9 = Trouble

BY CLAUDIA MILLS
ILLUSTRATED BY G. BRIAN KARAS
FARRAR, STRAUS & GIROUX, 2002. (I, U)

Wilson struggles to learn his third-grade multiplication tables. In contrast, his annoying younger brother seems to be having no trouble learning multiplication at all. But Wilson ultimately masters the times tables, just as he has overcome other challenges through hard work, planning, and patience. Children may pick out these themes when discussing how Wilson solves his dilemmas.

## Shrinking Violet

BY CARI BEST
ILLUSTRATED BY GISELLE POTTER
FARRAR, STRAUS & GIROUX, 2000. (P, I)

Shy and reserved, Violet hates to think of acting in the school play but finds the perfect backstage role and overcomes the class bully's teasing as well. The story emphasizes that everyone has something to contribute and that each person's wishes should be respected. Notice the way the illustrations point up individual differences and feelings.

## Surviving Brick Johnson

BY LAURIE MYERS
ILLUSTRATED BY DAN YACCARINO
CLARION, 2000. (U)

Afraid of being "maimed" by Brick, the biggest kid in his class, because of a cafeteria blunder, Alex takes all sorts of cautionary measures, such as enrolling in a karate class. But as Alex begins to see Brick in a variety of settings, including reading aloud to first graders and in the karate class, Alex is forced to reevaluate his image of Brick. This book will launch a lively discussion of the importance and accuracy of first impressions, the impact of stereotypes, and how we change our perception of others. This is a good book to pair with Andrew Clement's *The Jacket*, discussed in Chapter 9.

## The Talent Show

BY MICHELLE EDWARDS
HARCOURT, 2002. (I)

Howardina is excited to think that a local television station will be filming when she sings in her school talent show. But during dress rehearsal, the second grader panics and runs off the stage. The day is saved by her sensitive grandmother, who helps by not seeming to, and Howie's own resourceful way of pulling herself together. There's an additional page of advice for overcoming stage fright in this easy chapter book. (Series)

## Thank You, Mr. Falker

BY PATRICIA POLACCO
PHILOMEL, 1998. (P, I)

This autobiographical picture book tells how Tricia makes it all the way to fifth grade with a serious reading disability before a talented teacher finally gets her help. Tricia's view of herself as "dumb" will strike a note with many struggling readers, who may see hope in what she became—a talented writer and illustrator. Direct readers to Polacco's many factually based picture books, especially her photo-autobiography *Firetalking* (Richard C. Owen, 1994), which explains how she uses art and images to transmit timeless stories of diversity and humanity to children.

## Virgie Goes to School with Us Boys

BY ELIZABETH FITZGERALD HOWARD
ILLUSTRATED BY E.B. LEWIS
SIMON & SCHUSTER, 1999. (P, I)

Even though her older brothers must walk seven miles to the Quaker school, the sole school available to African-American children after the Civil War, little Virgie longs to join them. Readers will be intrigued to learn of the struggle for the universal right to an education. The author's concluding note, which connects this story to her own family history, offers another talking point.

## A Week in the Woods

BY ANDREW CLEMENT
SIMON & SCHUSTER, 2002. (U)

New to the school, Mark doesn't hit it off with his fifth-grade science teacher, Mr. Maxwell. Mark is from a wealthy family, resents his parents' move from Scarsdale, New York, and has low expectations of his new home in rural New Hampshire. Mr. Maxwell, in turn, has low expectations of Mark because of his privileged background. During the annual class campout in early spring, a potentially dangerous situation is averted, causing student and teacher to reassess their negative opinions of each other. Readers will have much to say about feeling defensive and the importance of second chances.

## Wemberly Worried

BY KEVIN HENKES
GREENWILLOW, 1999. (P)

Wemberly worries about all of the things that could happen before she finally gets to kindergarten and makes a friend. Note how the typeface and other illustrative hints indicate Wemberly's escalating anxiety. Among the many books with this theme are Jean Van Leeuwen's *Amanda Pig, School Girl* (Dial, 1997) and Miriam Cohen's *Will I Have a Friend?* (HarperCollins, 1967).

## The Year of Miss Agnes

BY KIRKPATRICK HILL
SIMON & SCHUSTER, 2000. (U)

A short novel set in 1948 Alaska shows what happens when a new teacher comes to Frederika's Athabascan village and tries to teach everyone in the one-room school house, including Fred's deaf sister, Bocca. While there are many cultural aspects of the tundra to notice and discuss, readers might be encouraged to ponder why most teachers left after a year and why Miss Agnes was willing to stay. They can talk about what made Miss Agnes a good teacher and what made the students good learners.

## Yoko

BY ROSEMARY WELLS
HYPERION, 1998. (P)

The first graders in Yoko the cat's class are quick to call her sushi lunch "yucky." But Yoko's teacher comes up with a plan to hold an International Food Day so that the students (each one is a different animal) in the class can share special food. While not everyone is convinced to try a new dish, Timothy tries Yoko's Japanese cuisine and each finds a friend. Pair with Russell Hoban's classic *Bread and Jam for Frances* (HarperCollins, 1964) and talk about food choices, individuality, and the challenge of trying new things. (Series)

# Hooked on
# Books

I admit it. I have a problem. Some people collect stamps, others collect coins or old albums. I collect books. From the ceiling to the floor, in shelves and on tables—they're everywhere. After 13 years of teaching, I've collected 3,000 children's books. So, when I read aloud to my kids every day, there's a great selection to choose from. Once a week, my students write me a letter about a book they've chosen, and I write them back. These letters help me connect with my students, not only about what they're reading, but also about what's happening in their lives.

DEBBI TEHRANI
JONES LANE ELEMENTARY SCHOOL
GAITHERSBURG, MARYLAND

Photo: Daniel Peck/PeckStudios

# Chapter 3

# Making Friends

Writer and philosopher Ralph Waldo Emerson had a lot to say about friends. A friend, he wrote, is "the masterpiece of nature," and he suggested, "One of the blessings of old friends is that you can afford to be stupid with them." (Norris, Boris, Morris, and Doris in Michele Sobel Spirn's wild and funny book, *The Know Nothings*, show just how true this is!) But Emerson also said, "The only way to have a friend is to be one," and this warmer side of friendship is portrayed in many of the books suggested here.

Having a friend and being a friend are an important part of growing up. Children view themselves as successful if they have friends, unsuccessful if they don't have them. Yet once secured, friendship is not without its difficulties, as young readers will learn when they explore the ups and downs of relationships in the books that follow. Is it fair to exclude one friend for the sake of another? Are bad friends better than no friends? What should you do when a friend betrays you?

Losing a friend is painful, too. Some friends, like Wilbur's beloved Charlotte, in the classic *Charlotte's Web* by E.B. White, are lost to old age or death. Some friends are lost by moving away or just moving on as Peter and Robert discover in Aliki's *Best Friends Together Again*. Regardless of the cause, not having a friend or losing a friend is a sadness almost everyone will experience.

Some unusual friendships transcend cultures, generations, even species. Look at the dog-and-boy stories in Cynthia Rylant's *Henry and Mudge* series or the unlikely friendship among cat, mouse, and cricket in George Selden's *The Cricket in Times Square*. Whenever, wherever friends find each other,

## Yo! Yes?

A book that always triggered conversations in our parent-child workshops was *Yo! Yes?* by Chris Raschka. When we asked parents to name the character their child would identify with, one father said his son was a Yo, the outgoing kid on the playground. A mother thought her daughter was a Yes, the shy one. Her daughter piped up, "Yeah, Mommy, that's me!" This book about friendship is very popular with the kids in our urban program because many of them identify with the Yo character—they say that Yo talks and acts like them. Our kids also appreciate and talk about how the book depicts children with very different personalities becoming friends.

**SHAYNA GRINDLE**
**PROGRAM COORDINATOR**
**TURNING THE PAGE PROGRAM**
**WASHINGTON, D.C.**

the fun can begin. Friends celebrate seasons, share memories, start clubs, and spend time together. They also figure out how to solve problems, negotiate compromises, and practice making their own needs known. Sometimes friends learn it's necessary to apologize, to let go of anger, and to make amends in words or in actions.

The strength, bravery, and risk taking that friendships engender can transform the world. Clover and Annie Rose climb over racial barriers—and the fence that divides them—in Jacqueline Woodson's pre-Civil Rights story, *The Other Side*. Two boys risk capture and death in the Civil War South to come to each other's aid in Patricia Polacco's family account, *Pink and Say*. And in Nazi-occupied Copenhagen, friendship sparks the courage and conviction Annemarie needs to spirit away her Jewish friend, Ellen, in Lois Lowry's *Number the Stars*.

The impact of friendships, those that are surprising and those that seem typical, can be amazing. As Frog and Toad, George and Martha, teammates Jackie Robinson and Peewee Reese, and Leslie and Jesse in *Bridge to Terebithia* all know, lives are forever changed by friendship.

**NIKKI GRIMES** *is an author and poet who paints in words much as a fine artist paints in pictures. Her characters and words stay with you long after you've turned the page or closed the book. Grimes is the author of **Talkin' About Bessie: The Story of Aviator Elizabeth Coleman**.*

**Your characters have been so real to the readers, one child even thought Danitra Brown was a friend of hers. How do you craft characters with such precision?**

Long ago, my father taught me to have a writer's eye and a writer's ear, to constantly listen and observe. I've spent my entire life doing just that—picking up a dialect, noticing an article of clothing or a delicate mannerism. Because I observe life, life is what ends up on the page.

# RECOMMENDED Books

P = Primary (Kindergarten – Grade 3)
I = Intermediate (Grade 3 – Grade 4)
U = Upper (Grade 4 – Grade 6)

## Annie Bananie and the Pain Sisters

BY LEAH KOMAIKO
ILLUSTRATED BY ABBY CARTER
DOUBLEDAY, 1998. (I)

When Bonnie and Annie Bananie start a new club called the Pain Sisters (one has had a broken bone, the other an appendix scar), Annie's best friend Libby becomes jealous and creates an imaginary problem. This fourth book about Annie Bananie launches discussion around excluding friends, jealousy, truthfulness, and friendly behavior. Kathleen Leverich addresses similar themes in her series for younger readers, one of which is *Best Enemies Forever* (illustrated by Walter Lorraine, Greenwillow, 1995). (Series)

## Best Friends Together Again

BY ALIKI
GREENWILLOW, 1995. (P, I)

Peter is nervous about his old friend Robert's first visit since he and his family moved to a new town. The boys are delighted to find that the bonds of friendship remain strong even though both have new buddies and new interests. The author sensitively handles the intimidation children feel when confronted with change. This book may help readers talk about their own attempts to remain connected with friends. Readers may also want to write letters, just like the two friends in the story. Peter and Robert were first introduced in Aliki's *We Are Best Friends* (Greenwillow, 1982).

## Bridge to Terebithia

BY KATHERINE PATERSON
HARPERCOLLINS, 1978. (U)

It seems unlikely that fifth grader Jesse would have a girl for a best friend. But when Leslie moves next door, that's just what happens. Leslie and Jesse share many interests, including their imagined woodland kingdom, Terabithia, which can be reached only by swinging over a gully. A sudden tragedy changes everything. The now-classic book asks children to explore how Jesse copes with the loss of a friend. Readers can discuss, too, the literal and metaphorical bridges Jesse crosses as a result of his friendship with Leslie.

## Charlotte's Web

BY E.B. WHITE
HARPERCOLLINS, 1952. (I, U)

When Fern saves the runt pig Wilbur, a spider named Charlotte befriends both and starts a series of events that ensure Wilbur's safety forever. This beautifully written and gentle fantasy not only introduces the cyclical nature of life but also demonstrates the power of friendship. This is one of the most frequently read-aloud stories to school-age children, so adults may wish to learn who has not yet heard or read this story before beginning.

## Chester's Way

BY KEVIN HENKES
MORROW, 1988. (P)

Chester and Wilson are best friends and like doing things the same way all the time. That is until Lilly moves to the neighborhood and likes to do things her way. The book suggests that there are different ways to be a loyal friend and readers will want to discuss the challenges of three-way friendships. A similar trio of friends is introduced in *Horace and Morris but Mostly Dolores* by James Howe, illustrated by Amy Walrod (Atheneum, 1999).

## Cool Crazy Crickets

BY DAVID ELLIOTT
ILLUSTRATED BY PAUL MEISEL
CANDLEWICK, 2000. (I)

What can four friends do during the summer? These friends form a club, name it, and find a place to house it. Readers may note how the children work out the organizational details and what becomes important in this club. Breezy writing and colorful line drawings give this book an inviting look for new readers. Some children might like to design a clubhouse or plan a club they'd like to join. (Series)

## The Cricket in Times Square

BY GEORGE SELDEN
ILLUSTRATED BY GARTH WILLIAMS
FARRAR, STRAUS & GIROUX, 1960. (I)

When Chester, a cricket, is transported from his Connecticut home to the New York subway, he befriends Harry and Tucker, a cat and mouse who live near the Bellinis' newsstand. Chester's musical skill and Harry and Tucker's knowledge of the city combine to help the human family when they're in trouble. In addition to contrasting city and country lifestyles, the unlikely friendship among Chester, Harry, and Tucker highlights how distinct personalities come together to create lasting friendships.

## Danitra Brown Leaves Town

BY NIKKI GRIMES
ILLUSTRATED BY FLOYD COOPER
HARPERCOLLINS, 2001. (P, I)

Danitra is sent to visit relatives in the country for the summer. Her best friend, Zuri, is left behind in the city. Readers may want to explore how friends feel when they are separated and what they can do to stay in touch. They might also discuss how poetry here changes the story content and our reaction to it. The girls are first introduced in *Meet Danitra Brown* (HarperCollins, 1994).

## Freak the Mighty

BY RODMAN PHILBRICK
SCHOLASTIC, 1993. (U)

Kevin (*aka* "Freak") is born with a birth defect that prevents him from growing. He befriends a gentle giant of a boy named Max. Together they become Freak the Mighty as Kevin rides on Max's shoulders, defying the bullies and helping Max cope with family problems. The author skillfully draws readers into the adventure of unlikely friendship, while quietly commenting on unreasonable expectations based on appearance— themes that will resonate with children. The story continues in *Max the Mighty* (Scholastic, 1998).

## Freedom Summer

BY DEBORAH WILES
ILLUSTRATED BY JEROME LAGARRIGUE
ATHENEUM, 2001. (P, I)

Best friends Joe and John Henry share many interests—especially swimming. But because Joe has skin the "color of pale moths" and John Henry's is "the color of browned butter," they can't swim together in the town's pool, even after passage of the 1964 Civil Rights Act that legally ends racial segregation. Readers will be as shocked as the boys when townspeople fill the pool with asphalt. Invite children to talk about the heroism of holding together friendship in hard times.

## Frog and Toad Are Friends

BY ARNOLD LOBEL
HARPERCOLLINS, 1979. (P)

Frog and Toad are caring friends. In each of the five short stories here, curmudgeonly Toad and stalwart and cheerful Frog demonstrate their camaraderie. Readers can discuss or list the many ways the two show how much they like each other. The last story in this classic book invites children to write a note to someone they care about, just as the generous Frog does for Toad. (Series)

## George and Martha

BY JAMES MARSHALL
HOUGHTON MIFFLIN, 1974. (P)

George and Martha are the best of friends, but
they don't always like the same things. So it's
only logical that to avoid hurting Martha's feelings, but also to avoid eating dreaded pea soup,
George pours it into his shoe. Uncomplicated line
drawings are as expressive and as humorous as
the understated text and give children neat clues
as to how these hippopotamus friends behave
when they disagree and also how each is aware
of the other's feelings. From here, it's a short hop
to talking about readers' own friends. (Series)

## Gold Dust

BY CHRIS LYNCH
HARPERCOLLINS, 2000. (U)

The friendship between Richard, a white boy
from a working class family, and Napoleon, the
dark-skinned son of a college professor from the
Caribbean, just barely survives the racial tension
in Boston of the mid-1970s. Richard decides that
the two of them should team up to play baseball
just like the Boston Red Sox's "Gold Dust Twins,"
Jim Rice and Fred Lynn. This obsessive dream
puts an almost unbearable burden on Napoleon,
who has other interests. Baseball figures
prominently in this fast-paced, sophisticated
novel of friendship between two very different
boys during tense times.

## Good Night, Mr. Tom

BY MICHELLE MAGORIAN
HARPERCOLLINS, 1982. (U)

Eight-year-old Willie Beech meets Thomas
Oakley when he's evacuated from London during
World War II. Though Willie is sent back to
London, Mr. Tom rescues him from an abusive
situation in a riveting but tough scene that
shows that the war isn't the only danger in
Willie's life. This book will inspire discussion of
intergenerational friendships and differences in
protection provided to children then and now.

## Harley

BY STAR LIVINGSTON
ILLUSTRATED BY MOLLY BANG
SEASTAR, 2001. (P, I)

Harley is a llama unlike others of his kind. In this
often humorous story, Harley befriends sheep and
defends them against marauding coyotes. Harley
is fiercely loyal but also fiercely independent—
characteristics of friends and friendship that
should make for a lively discussion.

## Helen Keller: Rebellious Spirit

BY LAURIE LAWLOR
HOLIDAY HOUSE, 2001. (U)

Primary sources are used to introduce Helen
Keller within the context of the time in which
she lived. Though blind, deaf, and mute, Helen
was very intelligent. Readers might talk about
how her teacher and friend, Anne Sullivan,
helped direct Helen's energy; the hardships the
two friends weathered; and whether Anne
benefited from her friendship with Helen.

## Holes

BY LOUIS SACHAR
FARRAR, STRAUS & GIROUX, 1998. (U)

When Stanley Yelnats is wrongly accused and
convicted of theft, he winds up at Camp Green
Lake, a juvenile detention center in the middle of
an arid Texas desert. Here he digs 5x5 holes with
other quirky characters, all underdogs. Parallel
stories in this contemporary tall tale explore
issues such as loyalty, friendship, and society's
castoffs with memorable, absurd humor. Readers
may need to talk frequently about what they're
discovering and what they predict will happen
to keep track of the many intriguing threads
brought together neatly in the story's conclusion.

## A Hundred Dresses

BY ELEANOR ESTES
ILLUSTRATED BY LOUIS SLOBODKIN
HARCOURT, 1944. (I)

Wanda Petronski wears the same faded dress to
school every day but claims she has a hundred at
home. She does, of course—Wanda has created
them in drawings for which she is eventually hon-
ored at school. But it's too late—Wanda's family
has left town to get away from the taunts and teasing. Maddie was almost Wanda's friend and might

have been more supportive of her. Readers can explore why Maddie behaved as she did, how she felt after Wanda and her family departed, and how Maddie could have been a better friend.

## Judy Moody

BY MEGAN MCDONALD
ILLUSTRATED BY PETER REYNOLDS
CANDLEWICK, 2000. (I)

Even a good-natured kid can get into a bad mood, especially when she has to start a new grade in a new school. Judy's various grumps are improved when she gets to make a "me" collage—an activity most children enjoy—and begins to make friends. The creative and independent Judy presents readers with various examples of how to make friends and how friends put up with each other's bad moods. Young readers will see themselves and others in this humorous book. (Series)

## Junie B., First Grader (at Last!)

BY BARBARA PARK
ILLUSTRATED BY DENISE BRUNKUS
RANDOM HOUSE, 2002. (I)

The irrepressible Junie comes to the aid of her adult friend in the cafeteria—with surprising and funny results! Readers may laugh at Junie's way of seeing things and compare Junie's school and its policies to their own elementary schools. They may also discuss what qualities of Junie's might make her a good friend to have. (Series)

## The Know Nothings

BY MICHELE SOBEL SPIRN
ILLUSTRATED BY R.W. ALLEY
HARPERCOLLINS, 1999. (P)

Morris, Boris, Norris and Doris have a tough time getting things right—except for their friendship. Their silly adventures will generate giggles and discussion about the literal meaning of things (are French fried potatoes only available in France?) within the context of loyal friendship. Some children may see parallels between The Know Nothings and Amelia Bedelia, Peggy Parrish's cheerful but often clueless maid. (Series)

## The Lost Ball/La Pelota Perdida

BY LYNN REISER
GREENWILLOW, 2002. (P)

Two boys—one who speaks English, the other Spanish—come together in the park after each loses a ball. Carefully crafted illustrations and bilingual text introduce readers to Richard and Ricardo as they meet each other. Note the visual devices used to depict the emerging friendship, which compares well with Chris Raschka's Yo, Yes! in Chapter 9. Reiser's Margaret and Margarita/Margarita y Margaret (Greenwillow, 1993) is similar in theme to The Lost Ball, as girls and their mothers become friends despite their language differences.

## Matthew and Tilly

BY REBECCA JONES
ILLUSTRATED BY BETH PECK
DUTTON, 1991. (P)

Best friends Matthew and Tilly share the simple pleasures of life in the city until the day they have an argument. This book is a good choice for talking about apologies, compromise, winning an argument at the cost of friendship, and what it takes to get along with others.

## Me, Mop and the Moondance Kid

BY WALTER DEAN MYERS
DELACORTE, 1988. (I)

The narrator, T.J., and his brother, Moondance, become friends with Mop—nicknamed for her hair—before they're all adopted and continue to be best friends. The book will trigger speculation about what interests two boys and a girl can share as friends and about situations in which compromise is necessary. The adventures of this threesome continue in Mop, Moondance and the Nagasaki Knights (Delacorte, 1992), in which the trio plays Little League baseball internationally.

## Mud Flat Spring

BY JAMES STEVENSON
GREENWILLOW, 1999. (P, I)

The residents of Mud Flat are ready for spring, except perhaps for Morgan, a bear, who wants to continue hibernating. The author gives each of the numerous animal characters its own name and particular style of behavior, which he depicts in short, comically illustrated chapters with a wry humor. Inhabitants of Mud Flat are much like residents of any small community. The Mud Flat stories can encourage not only exploration of friendship but also of how and why a community is formed. (Series)

## My Louisiana Sky

BY KIMBERLY WILLIS HOLT
HENRY HOLT, 1998. (U)

Tiger Ann, teased because of her mentally challenged parents, is devastated when her grandmother suffers a fatal heart attack. Themes of changing friendships, particularly with a boy, decision making, and loyalty are skillfully integrated in this memorable story set in the rural Louisiana of the 1950s. Readers might explore how loyalty to family affects or changes friendship.

## The Naked Lady

BY IAN WALLACE
ROARING BROOK PRESS, 2002. (P, I)

When Tom is asked to take a pie to the new owner of the farm next to his family's farm, he is extremely surprised to come across a classically rendered statue of a nude woman, tastefully depicted. He meets and befriends Pieter, the widowed artist who created the sculpture as a tribute to his wife. Tom comes to appreciate how Pieter's loneliness is eased by sculpting, just as readers can talk about how art helps them cope with difficult times. As befits a book about art, much of the blossoming friendship between Tom and Pieter is told through the illustrations. This story is based on the author's own experiences.

## New Neighbors for Nora

BY JOHANNA HURWITZ
ILLUSTRATED BY LILLIAN HOBAN
MORROW, 1979. (I)

Nora is a vivacious, curious child, with few children to play with in her building except her younger brother and four-year-old Russell. When neighbors move into her apartment building, Nora anxiously hopes for new playmates. These gently humorous short stories build to a theme on making friends and introduce big city apartment living to readers. A newly illustrated version by Debbie Tilley is also available. (Series)

## Number the Stars

BY LOIS LOWRY
HOUGHTON MIFFLIN, 1989. (I, U)

Annemarie Johansen and Ellen Rosen's bond takes on an entirely new meaning with the Nazi takeover of Copenhagen. Friendship provides both families with the courage and determination to get Ellen and her family to safety, away from those who hate them just because the Rosens are Jews. This Newbery Medal book is based on a true story, fictionalized by the author, and introduces a historical period as well as a remarkable and courageous friendship.

## The Other Side

BY JACQUELINE WOODSON
ILLUSTRATED BY E.B. LEWIS
PUTNAM, 2001. (P, I)

A fence and pre-Civil Rights discrimination separate Clover and Annie Rose—Clover is on one side, Annie Rose on the other. The stark white fence is a visual metaphor that divides the girls, though each clearly longs for the other's friendship. Talk with children about the emotional impact of the book's illustrations and what might happen when the girls cross the fence. Readers may also want to talk about other situations that can drive a wedge between friends and how friendship can overcome formidable obstacles.

## Pink and Say

BY PATRICIA POLACCO
PHILOMEL, 1994. (I, U)

During the Civil War, Pink, son of a slave from Georgia, saves Say, a white boy from Ohio. While recuperating at Pink's family home, Say teaches his new friend to read. The boys are captured and sent to Andersonville Prison, where Pink and many others die; Say lives to tell the story to future generations. Graceful text and illustration explore what tears people apart as well as what connects them. Readers can discuss how stories link generations, such as this tale handed down in the author's family. Polacco's poignant story in picture book format will be most appreciated by older readers with some knowledge of the Civil War.

## Poppleton and Friends

BY CYNTHIA RYLANT
ILLUSTRATED BY MARK TEAGUE
SCHOLASTIC, 1998. (P)

Poppleton the pig takes pleasure in his friends, Hudson, a mouse, and Cherry Sue, a llama, and decides that friendship is the key to happiness and long life. Hudson and Poppleton's day at the beach is complete only when they stop to tell Cherry Sue all about it. Cherry Sue eliminates Poppleton's fears of a massive dry-skin problem when she notices that his sweater is filled with lint. These gentle stories in short, easy-to-read chapters can be shared and discussed individually. Poppleton pairs well with books about Frog and Toad and George and Martha. (Series)

## P.S. Longer Letter Later

BY PAULA DANZINGER AND ANN M. MARTIN
SCHOLASTIC, 1998. (U)

This story, sorted out in each girl's distinct voice, chronicles how best friends, Tara*Starr and Elizabeth continue to support each other through family turbulence, even when one moves away. Readers particularly will enjoy talking about how the author depicts the girls' decidedly different personalities through the technique of correspondence. This friendship continues via e-mail in *Snail Mail No More* (Scholastic, 2000).

## Teammates

BY PETER GOLENBOCK
ILLUSTRATED BY PAUL BACON
HARCOURT, 1990. (I)

Jackie Robinson, the first African American to play major league baseball, demonstrated enormous courage as he stood up to the prejudice of fans and players. It also took courage for friend and teammate Peewee Reese to stand in support of Jackie Robinson at the 1947 game in Cincinnati when fans booed a "Negro" player. Note other acts of bravery by Branch Rickey and Robinson's family and friends who helped change baseball. Another catalyst for change in baseball was Mamie Johnson, whose story is told in *A Strong Right Arm: The Story of Mamie "Peanut" Johnson* by Michelle Green in Chapter 6.

## Thorndike and Nelson: A Monster Story

BY JEAN JACKSON
ILLUSTRATED BY VERA ROSENBERRY
DK PUBLISHING, 1997. (P)

Thorndike and Nelson are best friends and, like all best friends, they sometimes have disagreements. But being monsters, their behavior is absolutely horrid, until they figure out they may lose the most important thing of all, their friendship. Anger and monstrous behavior can flare up suddenly but children, like Thorndike and Nelson, can discuss how to defuse the situation and make amends.

## To Fly: The Story of the Wright Brothers

BY WENDIE OLD
ILLUSTRATED BY ROBERT ANDREW PARKER
CLARION, 2002. (I, U)

Famous for their flight over Kitty Hawk, Orville and Wilbur were not only problem solvers, they were brothers with amazingly complementary skills. This biography of the celebrated brothers focuses not only on their aspirations and accomplishments, but also on their close friendship and how it contributed to their achievements. Gather other biographies of this famous pair to see how photographers, different illustrators, and a variety of authors treat the same subject matter differently.

## The Traitor: Golden Mountain Chronicles, 1885

BY LAURENCE YEP
HARPERCOLLINS, 2003. (U)

Two boys from completely different backgrounds—one Chinese, the other Irish, each American—provide two voices to explore the meaning of friendship, prejudice, and survival. Their perspectives are presented in alternating chapters, providing a look at the lives of those who mined in the Wyoming Territory in 1885. Tension escalates as Chinese crews are brought in to replace western workers at lower wages. Though Joseph Young, a Chinese boy born in America, is on one crew and Michael Purdy is on an "American" crew, each boy comes to understand the other's point of view as their friendship gradually grows. (Series)

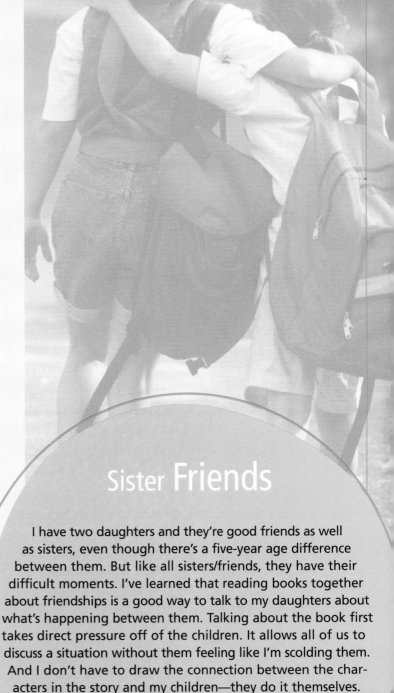

### Trout and Me

BY SUSAN SHREVE
KNOPF, 2002. (U)

Fifth grade for Ben is made bearable by Trout, Ben's first-ever friend. Both boys have attention deficit disorder and are clearly out of the mainstream in school. They also come from very different homes. One boy has the support of his parents and sister; the other boy rarely sees his parents. This story invites readers to explore the ways families help in the absence of friends and the joys and challenges of having a friend but losing him.

### When the Circus Came to Town

BY LAURENCE YEP
HARPERCOLLINS, 2002. (I,U)

After being permanently scarred by small pox, Ursula vows never to show her face in public again. But when Ah Sam, a Chinese cook who works at her family's stagecoach stop, creates a circus for the entire community, he helps restore Ursula's confidence. Set in Montana in the early 20th century, the book portrays the friendship between Ursula and Ah Sam as an unusual one, though they have much in common. Readers will empathize with Ursula's distress over her appearance and find the historical setting at once foreign and familiar.

### Wilfred Gordon McDonald Partridge

BY MEM FOX
ILLUSTRATED BY JULIE VIVAS
KANE MILLER, 1985. (P)

Wilfred Gordon lives next to a retirement home. When his favorite friend begins to lose her memory, Wilfred Gordon's caring actions help Miss Nancy Alison Delacourt Cooper remember. This is a good book to use to talk about how memories bind people together and how concern and affection may be shown for friends of any age.

## Sister Friends

I have two daughters and they're good friends as well as sisters, even though there's a five-year age difference between them. But like all sisters/friends, they have their difficult moments. I've learned that reading books together about friendships is a good way to talk to my daughters about what's happening between them. Talking about the book first takes direct pressure off of the children. It allows all of us to discuss a situation without them feeling like I'm scolding them. And I don't have to draw the connection between the characters in the story and my children—they do it themselves. In the end, my daughters always say, "That's what we did, didn't we?"

**CYNTHIA TAYLOR**
**PARENT OF A 12- AND 7-YEAR-OLD**

Chapter 4

# Connecting TO Communities

What is a community? "It's where we live," says Charlie in Judith Caseley's *On the Town: A Community Adventure*. In one sense, Charlie's right. A community is a network of people who share concerns in a common place. This place includes schools, stores, offices, churches, and other institutions that provide goods and services. But in a larger sense, "community" is not where we live, it's how we live. It's the agreements we make, the principles we share, the values we hold that bind us together in villages, towns, cities, and the world.

The definition of community includes smaller networks as well—a group of neighbors paints a mural in George Ancona's *Barrio: Jose's Neighborhood* or gathers for construction in Jane Yolen's *Raising Yoder's Barn*; a girl and her family in Karen Cushman's *The Ballad of Lucy Whipple* cook for California gold miners and create a settlement; a girls' baseball team in Virginia Euwer Wolff's *Bat Six* becomes an influence in a small town. These smaller groups support their members by helping them grow, by providing friendship, and by teaching the ways and beliefs that community holds dear. Communities provide the framework for this chapter, but readers will quickly come to understand that the varied individuals within those communities make them work.

When people get together around things they care about, whether it's cleaning up the playground, forming a group garden, saving a corner grocery store, or taking care of an injured cat, they are building community. What a child learns from neighborhood experiences like these is carried into the larger world. Many of the books presented here plant the idea that children can indeed make a difference in their communities, a theme that's also explored in Chapter 9.

# Bus
# Buddies

Being a member of a community isn't always easy, as many of the strong characters young readers will meet here know so well. When 12-year-old Casey moves to Chinatown to live with her grandmother in Laurence Yep's *Child of the Owl*, she feels out of step within her own culture. When Esperanza is uprooted from her family's Mexican ranch to work as a farm laborer—in *Esperanza Rising* by Pam Muñoz Ryan—she finds the nurturing support she needs in an unlikely place.

We were at our wit's end! What could our dedicated bus driver do about the discipline problems we were having with one busload of students who had a long bus ride each day? After conferring with the bus driver, I started Bus Buddies, a reading program that teamed older students with younger students. The younger buddies read the books, while the older children guided them through the book, asking about plot, setting, and other story elements. Each morning, the bus driver placed the books on the seats before the students got on, encouraging the buddies to get started right away. At the end of the week, the students received points toward their reading goals. The difference in the kids was like night and day, and everyone in the school community benefited from this innovative program. The bus driver loved the change in student behavior. Teachers were ecstatic that their students were accelerating their reading skills. Parents were pleased with their children's progress. The older buddies were happy to be leaders, and the younger buddies were excited to focus their attention on reading instead of tormenting one another!

**ALISON WARD**
**ASSISTANT PRINCIPAL**
**WRIGHTSBORO ELEMENTARY SCHOOL**
**WILMINGTON, NORTH CAROLINA**

Sometimes a tightly knit or well-defined community leaves a person no space in which to grow. Community values can confine behaviors, embarrass members, or cause conflict. Sometimes people feel isolated because they can't quite see how to fit into their community. Books for older readers—like Jill Paton Walsh's science-fiction chronicle, *The Green Book*, or Lois Lowry's futuristic fantasy, *The Giver*—deal with these issues head on.

The books in this chapter take readers into all sorts of diverse communities. Many stories celebrate community achievements, connectedness, and the support network that forms when people face disasters, hard times, disappointments, and misunderstandings. One poignant example is *Fireboat: The Heroic Adventures of John J. Harvey* by Maira Kalman, which tells of the restoration of a 1931 fireboat to help in the aftermath of September 11, 2001.

As they delve into and discuss the books in this chapter, children will find themselves irresistibly drawn into a very special sort of community—the community of readers.

**JACQUELINE WOODSON** *is an acclaimed author known for creating unforgettable characters who tackle the difficult issues young people face. Her books include* **Visiting Day, Miracle's Boys,** *and* **Hush**.

**Your stories put characters through tough situations but there is always a strong sense of identity and community in your books, even when your characters feel they're outsiders. Why is this important to you?**

Growing up, I often felt like the outsider. When I picked up a book, I didn't see people who looked like me or who came from the same neighborhoods I did. I decided that when I grew up, I would write about communities and people who were familiar to me. I would write about friendship and all the things I felt were missing in a lot of the books I read as a child. I want children to know it's okay to be yourself, no matter who you are in the world—and there will always be people who are there for you at different times in your life, even if you don't see that at first.

# RECOMMENDED Books

## The Ballad of Lucy Whipple

**BY KAREN CUSHMAN**
HOUGHTON MIFFLIN, 1996. (U)

When her family uproots from Massachusetts and moves to Gold Rush country in the late 1840s, California Morning Whipple protests by changing her name to Lucy. She fiercely objects to living in the raw camp settlement but as her family works to create a new town, Lucy discovers a talent for baking pies and a craving to read the few books available in camp. She later discovers her life's vocation based on her love of reading and becomes one of the territory's first librarians. Plenty of history underpins this story that invites readers to talk about how communities get their starts.

## Barrio: José's Neighborhood

**BY GEORGE ANCONA**
HARCOURT, 1998. (I)

This informational photo essay about San Francisco's Mission District is seen through the eyes of eight-year-old José. Friends, teachers, family celebrations, public murals, festivals, and street life all will resonate with the reader. By highlighting this colorful Latino neighborhood, the author provides a model for children to create their own illustrated tour, including the businesses, social services, educational facilities, and friends who give communities character and warmth. The power of public art in creating community is also captured in *Murals: Walls That Sing* (Cavendish, 2003) and in *The Piñata Maker* (Harcourt, 1994).

## Bat Six

**BY VIRGINIA EUWER WOLFF**
SCHOLASTIC, 1998. (U)

Individual voices from rival girls' softball teams in two Oregon towns gradually reveal the impact of World War II on their community. Each team has a "ringer," each American but with different war experiences: one girl and her family spent the war in a Japanese internment camp; the other lost her father in the attack on Pearl Harbor. Gradually, individual voices converge to create a community that questions what could have been handled differently in the ensuing team incidents. Readers may consider how individual decisions to act or not act can change the outcome of events and how communities are built through accumulations of such decisions.

## Because of Winn-Dixie

**BY KATE DICAMILLO**
CANDLEWICK, 2000. (I, U)

Opal Buloni, abandoned by her mother and raised by a single preacher father, adopts a dog she names after the supermarket from which she rescued it. Winn-Dixie gradually helps her make new friends in the small Florida town where candy can taste "sweet and sad" at the same time. This funny, gentle, and moving story lets readers talk about how everyone needs and can make friends, no matter what their ages.

### Black Cat

BY CHRISTOPHER MYERS
SCHOLASTIC, 1999. (I)

What does a black cat roaming the city see? What is it looking for? Sophisticated and energetic collages combine with rap-like text to explore the urban landscape. Younger readers may discuss the cat's journey, while older readers may want to talk about the art and the way the language captures the sometimes gritty rhythm of the city. Bryan Collier provides another glimpse of urban America in *Uptown* (Holt, 2000), as does Walter Dean Myers' *Harlem* (illustrated by his son, Christopher Myers, HarperCollins, 1997).

### Chato and the Party Animals

BY GARY SOTO
ILLUSTRATED BY SUSAN GUEVARA
PUTNAM, 2000. (P)

Chato the cat, introduced in *Chato's Kitchen* (Putnam, 1995), is worried about his "homecat," Novio Boy, who's depressed because he's never had a birthday party. So the cat and mouse community plan a party, but with a few surprises. Energetic pictures and lively text sprinkled with Spanish provide a springboard for discussion about how people celebrate birthdays and ways parties bring people together.

### Chicken Sunday

BY PATRICIA POLACCO
PHILOMEL, 1992. (P)

A Russian-American girl narrates the story of her friendship with neighborhood boys, Stewart and Winston, and their grandmother, Miss Eula, who practice a different religion and who are African American. The book invites readers to share stories about diversity in their own communities and consider how different traditions merge to enhance daily life. The author draws on her Russian heritage again in *Rechenka's Eggs* (Putnam, 1988) and explores her roots in her easy-to-read autobiography, *Firetalking* (photographs by Lawrence Migdale, Richard C. Owen, 1994).

### Child of the Owl

BY LAURENCE YEP
HARPERCOLLINS, 1977. (U)

In the mid-1960s, 12-year-old Casey knows little about her Chinese background and thinks of herself as American. So when she moves to Chinatown in San Francisco to live with her maternal grandmother, she feels alienated and isolated. Gradually, Casey comes to accept and understand her Chinese background. Readers will be moved by the theme of isolation within one's own culture and fascinated with the distinguishing features of this ethnic community. The book generates a good discussion about the challenges and rewards of living in two cultures.

### Deshawn Days

BY TONY MEDINA
ILLUSTRATED BY GREGORY CHRISTIE
LEE AND LOW, 2001. (I, U)

Though 10-year-old Deshawn Williams' neighborhood may be rough, his home is a sanctuary of warmth and safety. What makes it so cozy? Note how Deshawn's story, told in verse and illustrated with striking, angular, semi-abstract paintings, provides a sense of place. The story suggests to readers ways that Deshawn's family contributes to a sense of community.

### Dragonfly Tale

BY KRISTINE RODANAS
CLARION, 1992. (P)

An ancient Zuni story tells how the Ashiwi people were watched over by two powerful spirits. When the spirits came disguised as beggars, the community was cruel to them. So the spirits decided to teach the Ashiwi a lesson. Luckily, two children's generous gesture saves the tribe from famine. Tucked into the story is a tale on how the dragonfly came to be. Many Native American stories center on themes of community balance, thrift, kindness, and generosity in addition to explaining aspects of the natural world.

### Escaping to America: A True Story

BY ROSALYN SCHANZER
HARPERCOLLINS, 2000. (I)

In 1921, the Jewish Goodstein family abandons its home in Poland and moves to America. What forces people into such seemingly drastic action?

What difficulties do people have in establishing a new home in a new place? Readers can talk about the ways this extended family helped each member escape from Europe and settle in a Tennessee community. This story is based on the author's family history and would contrast well with the similarly themed but contemporary *Marianthe's Story* by Aliki in Chapter 2.

## Esperanza Rising

BY PAM MUÑOZ RYAN
SCHOLASTIC, 2000. (U)

Esperanza's privileged life ends with her father's death. She and her family leave their Mexican ranch to work as farm laborers in an arduous California camp where her new—though initially despised—community provides support and help when most needed. This story, narrated by Esperanza, introduces the essence of community in the context of the Depression in the 1930s and within another culture, the migrant camps of Mexican Americans. See also a vibrant nonfiction book chronicling the creation of a school in the same setting: *Children of the Dust Bowl: The True Story of the School at Weed Patch Camp* by Jerry Stanley (Crown, 1992).

## Fireboat: The Heroic Adventures of John J. Harvey

BY MAIRA KALMAN
PUTNAM, 2002. (P, I)

This hopeful picture book encompasses many communities as it tells the story of a fireboat built in 1931 that responds to the attacks of September 11, 2001. The boat served well, was abandoned, and then rehabilitated by a group of interested citizens. It was brought out of retirement to help during heroic rescue efforts at the World Trade Center. This is a great book for discussing the interplay of individual and community, since the efforts of a few preservationists enabled this boat to serve greater New York. Children will be captivated by the description of the working fireboat and its many parts. But some may be frightened by the tragedy carefully but explicitly pictured. For that reason, younger readers might do well reading the book alongside a grown-up friend.

## The Four Ugly Cats in Apartment 3D

BY MARILYN SACHS
ILLUSTRATED BY ROSANNE LITZINGER
ATHENEUM, 2002. (I)

Ten-year-old Lily takes responsibility for four cats when a crotchety neighbor dies in apartment 3D and leaves them homeless. Lily's plan to find a place for each cat takes her into the neighborhood and the reader into a variety of encounters and settings. Information about cats is cleverly worked into the story and might inspire some children to research cat breeds or visit the local animal shelter. Lily's artful persuasion of potential cat owners should make for a lively discussion of how readers would go about solving a dilemma in their own neighborhoods.

## Frederick

BY LEO LIONNI
RANDOM HOUSE, 1967. (P)

Frederick sits on a rock and gathers colors while the other mice work and call to him to help bring in the harvest. "I do work," he says. "I gather sun rays…colors…words." So when the cold winter comes, Frederick's poems kindle memories of spring and warm the community. Lionni's *Swimmy* (Random House, 1963) shows how small fish can live among big fish by using their collective wits. Both books encourage readers to talk about the value of diversity in a strong community.

## The Giant Carrot

BY JAN PECK
ILLUSTRATED BY BARRY ROOT
DIAL, 1998. (P)

What does it take to extract a huge carrot from the garden? It takes the cooperation of the whole community. This folktale has been retold with enormous turnips or huge potatoes, all needing to be pulled out by an accumulating group of characters. Numerous folktales present a puzzle and then add one character after another until the problem is finally solved. This tried-and-true formula makes for wonderful group discussions, with each reader speaking for a different person in the story. Young children can easily dramatize this cumulative story with very few props. Another folktale with the same cooperative theme is Ed Young's *Seven Blind Mice* (Philomel, 1992).

## The Giver

BY LOIS LOWRY
HOUGHTON MIFFLIN, 1993. (U)

Jonas lives in the future in a society that values sameness and predictability. He understands that, as is the custom, he will be assigned an adult job when he becomes a teenager. Still, he's shocked when he receives the overwhelming task of preserving the community's memories. As Jonas learns something of the world's history, he begins to question the underlying values of his society. This challenging fantasy offers readers a chance to discuss utopias, the responsibilities choice bestows, the use of language, and the role of memory. Readers will enjoy debating the enigmatic ending to see if they can agree on what will happen next.

## Goggles

BY EZRA JACK KEATS
MACMILLLAN, 1969. (P)

When Peter and his friend find a pair of old motorcycle goggles that inspire their imaginative play, they must protect their find from neighborhood bullies who want the treasure for themselves. Peter's dog Willie snatches the goggles and retreats to a hiding place, thus saving the day. Keats explores another aspect of urban life in *Apt. 3* (Macmillan, 1983), where the sounds in his building lead Sam and his brother on a quest that ends in apartment 3. These books invite readers to mentally explore urban neighborhoods, meet a community of children, and examine how Keats, a noted illustrator, used paper collage to portray the city landscape.

## Grandpa's Corner Store

BY DYANNE DISALVO-RYAN
HARPERCOLLINS, 2000. (I)

After a big hardware store opens and a giant supermarket announces plans to move into the neighborhood, Lucy discovers her grandfather is thinking of closing his small, community grocery store. She convinces him not to sell out by showing him how much his store means to the numerous families who live nearby. Celebration of community and neighborhood cohesiveness can also be found in the author's other titles, such as *Uncle Willie and the Soup Kitchen* (Morrow, 1991) and *The Castle on Viola Street* (HarperCollins), discussed in Chapter 9.

## The Green Book

BY JILL PATON WALSH
FARRAR, STRAUS & GIROUX, 1982. (I)

Readers will be delighted to recognize at the end of the story the book's beginning sentence, "Father said we could take very little with us." As the space ship takes off from Earth before the "disaster," Pattie is ridiculed for her impractical choice of a blank book. But then she uses it to chronicle the settlement of a new planet—the very chronicle children are reading in this story. This well-written book will get readers talking about the strengths and sacrifices needed to start a new community and makes the case that the communal need for storytelling is most powerful.

## Gus and Grandpa and the Christmas Cookies

BY CLAUDIA MILLS
ILLUSTRATIONS BY CATHERINE STOCK
FARRAR, STRAUS & GIROUX, 1997. (P)

Each winter, Gus and his grandfather spend time together baking cookies for the neighbors. This year, an excess of cookies causes them to take extras to the homeless shelter. This easy-reader chapter book is a good springboard for talking about things a child can do with an elderly relative as well as community institutions that support the needy and ways people in the community can contribute. There are many other stories about this "team" and the community in which they live. (Series)

## I'll Meet You at the Cucumbers

BY LILIAN MOORE
ILLUSTRATED BY SHARON WOODING
ATHENEUM, 1988. (I)

Adam, a country mouse, shares his love for nature with his mouse pen-pal, Amanda, who lives in the city. When he visits his friend, however, he is nearly overwhelmed by all the city has to offer until Amanda shows him the library and the many wonderful stories humans have written about mice. In addition, she convinces him that his letters are really poetry when she reads aloud a poem by Valerie Worth. The gentle story skirts the issue of which neighborhood is best in order to deal with the larger theme of new experiences and the way poetry lets us see the world from a fresh perspective. This chapter book compares well with a modern update of the old Aesop fable, told in

*Bernelly & Harriet: The Country Mouse and the City Mouse* by Elizabeth Dahlie (Little, Brown, 2002), for talking about the merits and challenges of rural and urban living.

## I Stink

### BY KATE AND JIM MCMULLAN
JOHANNA COTLER BOOKS/HARPERCOLLINS, 2002. (P)

Exuberant, varied typefaces and bold illustrations reflect a trash truck's pride in the important work it does. An alphabet of trash makes the point that without this city service, "you're on Mount Trash-o-rama, baby." Pair this with Andrea Zimmerman's chantable, rhyming *Trashy Town* illustrated by Dan Yaccarino (HarperCollins, 1999) to begin a discussion of city services in your area. Since neither book deals with recycling, you may wish to introduce this topic to the discussion.

## The Little House

### BY VIRGINIA LEE BURTON
HOUGHTON MIFFLIN, 1942. (P)

A little house in the country watches as the city gradually moves out to envelop her. This now classic book chronicles an experience that has changed many communities. Note the illustrations of lavish open circles that are gradually cluttered and cut by upthrusting buildings and the way the Little House is visually strangled by the elevated railway. Children may be inspired to map their own neighborhoods, compare the look of their neighborhood now to an earlier time, and discuss the impact of growing cities.

## The Little Painter of Sabana Grande

### BY PATRICIA MALONEY MARKUN
ILLUSTRATED BY ROBERT CASILLO
BRADBURY, 1993. (P)

In the mountains of Panama, Fernando makes his own paints with directions from his teacher. Since he has no paper, he paints the side of his house and soon the neighbors wish for their houses to be decorated, too. Based on a true story, the book evokes a discussion of public murals and other decorations people have created or could create to beautify their communities.

## Madlenka

### BY PETER SÍS
FOSTER/FARRAR, STRAUS & GIROUX, 2000. (P)

Madlenka has lost a tooth and circles "the world," her multicultural city neighborhood, to tell everyone, including shopkeepers, the newsstand man, and the baker. The illustrations zoom in, moving from universe, planet, continent, and country to city, block, and apartment. This charming character continues to explore the community in *Madlenka's Dog* (Foster/Farrar, 2002). Both books invite readers to draw posters of their own neighborhoods, identifying important people and places.

## Music, Music for Everyone

### BY VERA B. WILLIAMS
MORROW, 1984. (P)

Rosa, the girl introduced in *A Chair for My Mother* (see Chapter 1), and her friends plan The Oak Street Band to raise money for her sick grandmother's medical expenses. Be sure to notice the picture borders and the small complementary illustrations that Williams uses to emphasize important parts of the story. Children will enjoy talking about the connection between analyzing the pictures and reading the words. This heartwarming book will also get readers talking about community yard sales, dinners, fix-up days, and other fund-raisers that help people who need assistance.

## On the Town: A Community Adventure

### BY JUDITH CASELEY
GREENWILLOW, 2002. (P)

Charlie's homework is to keep a pictorial journal of people in his community. His pictures and labels introduce the people he and his mother meet as they go about their errands: barbers, postal clerks, police, restaurant staff, bankers, and neighbors. This book is guaranteed to spark a conversation about the people children meet as they wander through their own communities. And it's a smooth move from having conversations about Charlie's project to asking readers to create picture journals of their own.

## Powwow

BY GEORGE ANCONA
HARCOURT, 1993. (I)

In photo-essay format, Ancona presents a huge inter-tribal gathering in Crow, Montana. Readers attend the powwow in the company of Anthony Standing Rock, who goes from being a gawky kid to a warrior-dancer. But the real focus is the preparation and pride of ritual that unites the many tribes that attend this ceremony. Children will be fascinated with the four types of dances photographed—Traditional, Fancy, Grass, and Jingle-dress—and will be able to relate to the many small family rituals that are part of the event. Author Diane Hoyt-Goldsmith and photographer Lawrence Migdale have also focused on other Native American communities, in books such as *Lacrosse: The National Game of the Iroquois* (1998) and *Apache Rodeo* (1995, both Holiday House).

## Raising Yoder's Barn

BY JANE YOLEN
ILLUSTRATED BY BERNIE FUCHS
LITTLE, BROWN, 1998. (P, I)

After his family's barn is destroyed in a fire, Matthew Yoder tells how the Amish gather to rebuild the structure in a single day. Yolen's graceful text explores the meaning of community and Fuchs' warm watercolors glow. What does it take to pull off such a huge group project? Readers will discover the answer as they talk about who does what over the course of the day. Craig Brown's simpler *Barn Raising* (Greenwillow, 2002) provides children with a chance to compare two differing treatments of the same event. Readers might discuss how large community events, such as commemorative celebrations, family reunions, or club award ceremonies, are planned and organized by many people working toward a common goal.

## See You Around, Sam

BY LOIS LOWRY
ILLUSTRATED BY DIANE DEGROAT
HOUGHTON MIFFLIN, 1996. (I)

In this short novel, four-year-old Sam decides to run away to Alaska because his mother won't let him wear his plastic fangs. As he stops at neighbors' houses to say goodbye, he gets lots of advice and heavy but useful things to carry along. When the neighbors gather for a potluck supper, Sam is happy that he didn't get far from home. This is a great choice for middle elementary children to read on their own, and they'll appreciate the neighborhood network that—oh so casually—takes care of Sam without his knowledge. Discuss what contributes to Sam's gradual change of mind and how people in this community help him. (Series)

## Stone Soup

BY MARCIA BROWN
SCRIBNERS, 1947. (P)

This timeless classic conveys what happens when formerly selfish people begin to work together to create a group soup that feeds everyone. The illustrator's use of rust, black, and brown to portray the French setting, the wary peasants, and the weary soldiers gives this story a rustic look and a cozy feeling. Discuss why the villagers might have been selfish and what qualities of the soldiers convinced them to contribute. Jon J. Muth's telling of *Stone Soup* (Scholastic, 2003) is set in a northern Chinese village and blends a Buddhist story tradition of trickster monks who spread enlightenment. Comparison of the two stories shows how the bare bones of a folktale can be enriched by additions. The story itself invites children to think of events in the community that feed large groups of people.

## Three Cheers for Catherine the Great

BY CARI BEST
ILLUSTRATED BY GISELLE POTTER
DK PUBLISHING, 1999. (P)

Sara has a problem. Her Russian grandmother wants no presents for her birthday. This hardly seems fair, considering all the generous and thoughtful things her grandmother does every day for Sara and all the neighbors in the apartment building. Then inspiration hits. Sara and the neighbors decide to combine their individual talents and spend the big day in acts of generosity. Readers will delight in thinking up their own gifts from the heart and talking about warm relationships between older and younger people in their own neighborhoods.

## Uncle Jed's Barbershop

BY MARGAREE KING MITCHELL
ILLUSTRATED BY JAMES E. RANSOME
SIMON & SCHUSTER, 1993. (I)

It's the segregated South in the 1920s. Uncle Jed spends every Wednesday evening at Sarah Jean's house. As the only African-American barber in town, Uncle Jed often tells his young niece about his dream of opening his own barbershop some day. But when Sarah Jean needs an operation, Uncle Jed lends the money. A bank failure takes the rest of his savings. Finally, after waiting most of his life, Uncle Jed opens his own barbershop. Just as he helped his family and people in the community many times over the years, they turn out to help him celebrate "his dream come true." This is a great story for talking about plans or dreams for the future and what it takes to achieve them

## Yard Sale

BY MITRA MODARRESSI
DORLING KINDERSLEY, 2000. (P, I)

People in the imaginary rural town of Spudville keep to themselves until they all show up at a yard sale, where the magical properties of the purchases turn everyone into friends. This is an excellent book for talking about the real-life useful, enjoyable, and social outcomes of yard sales, garage sales, jumble sales, or whatever name they are called in your region. Have children bring in used items or books to exchange, or hold a neighborhood sale to benefit some aspect of their community. Compare this book to *Ragsale* by Artie Ann Bates (illustrated by Jeff Chapman-Crane, Houghton Mifflin, 1995), which sets this event in Appalachia.

Photo: Scott Suchman/NEA

# Chapter 5

# Looking AT THE World

Gaze into a kaleidoscope. See how the various bits of shaped glass, bright beads, and angled mirrors move together to form fascinating images? With a simple shift—a change in point of view—new images are created more beautiful than the last.

So it is when children learn to view the world in all its beauty, complexity, and diversity. A shift from the familiar—into the geography, culture, and experiences of another—offers children a new perspective and connects them to a broader world. Books that explore the world give children a new way of seeing.

Like the swirling of shapes in a kaleidoscope, the pattern of life today is one of delicate interconnection. The music we listen to, movies we watch, food we eat, and clothes we wear join us to the world community. We connect to the worldwide community through patterns in immigration, the way we treat our natural environment, health issues that affect us all, and the use of the world's resources.

While we hope today's children better appreciate diversity and understand our interconnectedness more than in times past, we recognize that children often see these differences as exotic or strange. Static stereotypes and gross generalizations about others create a limited view, which can translate into hurtful attitudes and actions. Yet we know that children, indeed all of us, need to form opinions from first-hand knowledge. The best children's books help supply this knowledge as young readers come to understand and connect with the experiences of others.

The books in this chapter are about contemporary people living in other parts of the world or people who are a part of some minority living within the United States. Often culturally specific, these books are written or illustrated by someone with "insider knowledge" of the customs. Mari Takabayashi glimpses life through the eyes of a second grader in *I Live in Tokyo*. George Ancona focuses the lens on present-day Cuba in *Cuban Kids*. Through story and picture details, the books reveal differences in geography, flora or fauna, occupations, family life, and cultural details. Most important, they connect young readers with the concerns of the child at the center of the story.

## Children Around the World

The cultural landscape is very different for my daughters than it was for my wife and me when we were growing up. My daughters attend school with children whose families come from around the world, so we started early introducing them to other cultures through books. They've read stories about children who live in Cambodia, Russia, Nigeria, Senegal, China, Poland, Mexico, and many other countries. These stories have given our daughters a point of reference for the people they meet, the cuisines they eat, and the events that take place around the world. And having this point of reference has helped them develop an appreciation—and tolerance—for cultures that are different from theirs.

**HARRY PUTMAN**
PARENT OF A **17-, 13-,** AND **9-YEAR-OLD**

A handful of these books point out the stunning diversity of the world at large. *Market!* by Ted Lewin celebrates markets as gathering places. Yann Arthus-Bertrand's aerial photographs in *Earth from Above for Young Readers* pull in to show an acre of rugs in a Morocco market and a glimpse of a single acacia tree in Kenya. In Barbara Brenner's *Voices: Poetry and Art from Around the World*, text and art combine to point out the beauty and similarities in people all over the world, even as we celebrate differences and diversity.

Because books have the ability to shape a child's worldview, those that present accurate, authentic information are highly valued. An author who has lived in a country or culture, or who has visited many times in an effort to understand and meet people before telling a story, helps authenticate the text. An illustrator who notes that he or she sketched and painted scenes on site, or did extensive research, lets children know that the book presents an authentic picture. If the book's creator comes from within the culture, readers can be reasonably sure that the story between the covers can be trusted.

It's important to discern authenticity and accuracy in text and illustration yourself and to discuss this with children. Guide them in looking for the credentials of a book's creators. Tell them to read the notes and back matter. Invite them to look at the jacket flaps. When you do, you're helping them develop critical evaluation skills, dispel stereotypes, and keep their minds open to diversity.

Children need maps and atlases to locate countries and continents and to help make the study of geography transparent. There are still too few excellent trade books and stories about contemporary life in other countries, and many go out of print rapidly as countries undergo change and the book's information grows less reliable. Selections here do not equally represent areas, countries, or cultures around the world. This is a short book, and the world is a big place!

Yet, while no single book—or a selection of books—can even begin to touch this topic, the books discussed here represent many different approaches, styles, and contexts for young readers to look at the world around them. Shift the kaleidoscope and enjoy the view.

**PAT MORA,** *a prolific writer of poetry and books for children, young adults, and adults, is known for her colorful style and books that celebrate the American and Latino culture.* **Tomás and the Library Lady; Confetti,** *a bilingual poetry collection; and the picture book biography,* **A Library for Juana: The World of Sor Juana Inés,** *show her diversity as an author. Here Mora talks about the importance of language and culture in books for children.*

**Many of your books are published in two languages, Spanish and English. Who decides if a book is printed in different languages, and why is that important?**

It's usually the publisher who's open to publishing the bilingual versions of my book. But I want to make sure that educators know those bilingual books are not just for the children who speak Spanish. They're as much for the non-Spanish-speaking children because these books open up the world to them. We need to celebrate the languages of our children in our schools and communities and encourage them to share with each other and the grownups. Books build bridges of culture and language with words as their gateways.

# RECOMMENDED Books

P = Primary (Kindergarten – Grade 3)
I = Intermediate (Grade 3 – Grade 4)
U = Upper (Grade 4 – Grade 6)

## Apple Pie 4th of July

BY JANET WONG
ILLUSTRATED BY MARGARET CHODOS-IRVIN
HARCOURT, 2002. (P)

"No one wants Chinese food on the Fourth of July," a Chinese-American girl tells her parents. But when the parade goes by, people are hungry and flock to the restaurant for an evening meal. By nightfall, the tired family rests on their roof and watches fireworks—sharing a neighboring family's apple pie. Discuss the evidence of two cultures blending in this book and note other ways different cultures contribute to diversity in your own community.

## Birthdays Around the World

BY MARY D. LANKFORD
ILLUSTRATED BY KAREN DUGAN
HARPERCOLLINS, 2002. (P, I, U)

This lively nonfiction book describes birthday celebrations in Mexico, New Zealand, Sweden, Malaysia, the Netherlands, and other countries. In addition, a chart shows what gems, flowers, and character traits are associated with a particular birth month. Children might enjoy comparing their own birthday traditions with those of others. A class party for all of those with summer birthdays might be celebrated with traditions borrowed

from the seven areas described here. The author has also written books about playing hopscotch, jacks, and dominoes around the world.

## Celebrating Ramadan

BY DIANE HOYT-GOLDSMITH
PHOTOGRAPHS BY LAWRENCE MIGDALE
HOLIDAY HOUSE, 2001. (I)

As in other books by this author and photographer, readers meet a child and his family, his neighborhood and friends, and follow him through the month-long celebrating of Ramadan. Books such as *Pueblo Storyteller* (1991), *Celebrating Quinceañera: A Latina's Fifteenth Birthday* (2002), and *Potlatch: A Tsimshian Celebration* (1997; all Holiday House) introduce contemporary American children who embody two cultures and also invite readers to consider America's diversity.

## Cuban Kids

BY GEORGE ANCONA
MARSHALL CAVENDISH, 2000. (I)

Photojournalist Ancona shows present-day Cuban children going to school in uniform, living with close-knit families in neighborhoods, and participating in community activities. Without touching on the politics of Cuban-American relationships, his pictures speak volumes. Notice the handmade books that serve the schools, and read the pictures for what the text doesn't state. There are few children's books about Cuba, and this one is a fine introduction to our neighbor.

## Earth from Above for Young Readers

PHOTOGRAPHS BY YANN ARTHUS-BERTRAND
TEXT BY ROBERT BURLEIGH
HARRY N. ABRAMS, 2001. (I, U)

A singularly beautiful collection of aerial photographs calls attention to variety in the world: in work, people, geography, patterns, nature, and colors. Burleigh's short paragraphs alert readers to detail and explain what you're seeing: an acre of rugs at a carpet market in Morocco or a lone acacia tree in Kenya surrounded by paths animals take to rest in its shade. The photographs inspire marvel, close inspection, and discussion. A map at the beginning helps children place the image geographically and begin to visualize other parts of the world.

## Encantado: Pink Dolphin of the Amazon

BY SY MONTGOMERY
PHOTOGRAPHS BY DIANNE TAYLOR-SNOW
HOUGHTON MIFFLIN, 2002. (U)

In a unique blend, this nonfiction book introduces the people living along the Amazon River even as it interests readers in the elusive freshwater dolphins the author has studied. "You're traveling to a world that is full of water," states the author, and we are also drawn into her methods of scientific inquiry. Like other Montgomery nonfiction books, this one works on many levels and the back matter, including a note on how the book was researched, is not to be missed.

## Families

BY ANN MORRIS
PHOTOGRAPHS BY KEN HEYMAN
HARPERCOLLINS, 2000. (P)

Selecting photographs from around the world, the author shows in minimal text how families look, what they do together, the games children and parents play, and the kinds of houses they live in, and lets the reader draw conclusions. Some of those might be that families love their children all over the world, that everyone plays, that all babies need care. The astute observer can read the pictures for interesting cultural details as well. A key tells the setting of each picture. There are many books in this series that demand close looking and generalization skills. (Series)

## Home at Last

BY SUSAN MIDDLETOWN ELYA
ILLUSTRATED BY FELIPE DÁVALOS
LEE & LOW, 2002. (P, I)

Since moving to the United States from Mexico, Ana Patina has started school, Papa has a job, and both are learning English. But not Mama, who is cheated at the grocery store because the clerk doesn't understand her. Only when one of Ana's twin brothers becomes ill does Mama decide to go to night school and learn English, too. Then she can make herself understood, straighten out the clerk, and make Ana proud of her efforts. The story mirrors the difficulty some family members have in learning a new language along with the many responsibilities children shoulder in a move. It invites talk about brave things parents have done and the challenges of moving to a new country.

## How My Parents Learned to Eat

BY INA FRIEDMAN
ILLUSTRATED BY ALLEN SAY
HOUGHTON MIFFLIN, 1984. (P)

The young narrator is as comfortable eating with chopsticks as she is with fork and knife, but that wasn't always the case for her parents. The straightforward text and clear illustrations describe how her parents, an American sailor and a Japanese student, met in Japan and fell in love, and tried in secret to learn to eat with unfamiliar utensils. Simultaneously humorous and wise, this slim book deals with cultural differences as well as similarities through the universal importance of table manners.

## If the World Were a Village: A Book about the World's People

BY DAVID J. SMITH
ILLUSTRATED BY SHELAGH ARMSTRONG
KIDS CAN PRESS, 2002. (U)

With over six billion people on the planet, it's difficult for children to generalize about populations. But this book imagines there are just 100 people. Then, 22 of us speak Chinese, 17 cannot read and write, and only 24 people have enough to eat, even though there are 189 chickens. Some pages would translate perfectly to child-made graphs to revisit the information. There's much for children to process, but the book's end matter presents several ideas that invite readers to develop a global overview.

## I Live in Tokyo

BY MARI TAKABAYASHI
HOUGHTON MIFFLIN, 2001. (I)

Mimiko, a second grader, tells the reader many things about her country over a year. She shares cultural details, festivals, everyday doings, Japanese words, customs, and other things important to children. It's a good introduction that can reinforce a study of Japan or allow a small group of children to become insider reporters. A handy last page offers numbers, phrases, words, and the months of the year in Japanese. The book pairs well with the informative *A to Zen* by Ruth Wells, illustrated by Yoshi (Simon & Schuster, 1992).

## Jakarta Missing

BY JANE KURTZ
GREENWILLOW, 2001. (U)

When 12-year-old Dakar and her parents move from east Africa to North Dakota, she feels like an outsider once again. She's even more isolated this time, however, because her older sister, Jakarta, has chosen to remain at boarding school. Dakar tells stories of her life in Africa, a place quite different than the middle of the United States. How Dakar struggles to understand herself, her family, and her new home and find her place in each is mitigated by her involvement on the basketball team and the process of growing up.

## Just Like Home/Como en Mi Tierra

BY ELIZABETH I. MILLER
ILLUSTRATED BY MIRA REISBERG
ALBERT WHITMAN, 1999. (P)

In Spanish and in English a girl compares aspects of her house, food, neighborhood, and school in her former country and in the United States. The phrases "not like home" or "just like home" mark her transition finally to "at home" in her new culture. A glossary reviews Spanish and English words, and the story acknowledges what children do naturally in new experiences—compare the former with the present.

## Learning to Swim in Swaziland: A Child's Eye View of a Southern African Country

BY NILA K. LEIGH
SCHOLASTIC, 1993. (I)

The author was an eight-year-old girl at the time she wrote these letters and illustrated journal entries about her year in Swaziland. It includes wonderful artwork with diagrams and labels, and personal observations about food, clothing, vocabulary, and customs. This unusual insider's look at an African country also serves as a writing model for classroom social studies of other countries.

## Market!

BY TED LEWIN
LOTHROP, LEE & SHEPARD, 1996. (I)

What happens in a marketplace? Lewin's watercolors capture marketplaces in Ecuador, Uganda, Ireland, New York, and other places where people buy and sell goods. Talk about places in the community where people gather to exchange goods. What do the shops look like—large or small, personal or impersonal—and why are they different? Discussing specific attributes of a place helps provide readers with a basis for comparisons.

## The Most Beautiful Place in the World

BY ANN CAMERON
ILLUSTRATED BY THOMAS B. ALLEN
KNOPF, 1988. (I, U)

Abandoned by his parents, seven-year-old Juan is being raised by his grandmother in Guatemala. But Juan benefits from her firm expectations and his growing competence. The themes of making your own life worthwhile, the dignity of work, the value of knowing how to read, and how people show they love you make this a powerful discussion book on many levels.

## My Chinatown: One Year In Poems

BY KAM MAK
HARPERCOLLINS, 2002. (I, U)

Evocative poems combine with highly realistic, full-page paintings to reveal one boy's transition from Hong Kong to his new home in New York's Chinatown. He gradually comes to adjust to, even celebrate, his new home from one winter to the next. His year ends where it began, on "New Year's Day!" when Chinatown is celebrated exuberantly. The difficulty of leaving one home for another is a universal experience, which can be discussed here in the specifics of the Chinese culture.

## Nadia's Hands
BY KAREN ENGLISH
ILLUSTRATED BY JONATHAN WEINER
BOYDS MILLS PRESS, 1999. (I)

Nadia doesn't truly want her hands painted with *mendhi* for her Auntie's traditional Pakistani wedding, but because she's the bridesmaid, she agrees. While she worries what her schoolmates will think of her patterned hands, she decides she's proud of them and may talk about them during show-and-tell time. The quiet story points out how some people may feel bicultural conflicts, but that traditions from a previous setting may translate just fine to a new one.

## 19 Varieties of Gazelle: Poems of the Middle East
BY NAOMI SHIHAB NYE
GREENWILLOW, 2002. (U)

Stating in her preface that "poetry slows us down," Nye offers this moving and thoughtful collection of poems that presents people from her own ethnic background and whose lives in the Middle East have something to tell us. The poetry deals with specific events but universal emotions to suggest commonalities between cultures. Readers can explore what the poet has experienced to create these poems, as well as what they evoke (and why). Don't miss the essential titles placed sideways on the page.

## Other Side of Truth
BY BEVERLY NAIDOO
HARPERCOLLINS, 2001. (U)

Twelve-year-old Sade and her younger brother, 10-year-old Femi, flee their Nigerian home when those seeking to kill their journalist father murder their mother. Abandoned in London by the woman who is paid to take them to their uncle, the children wind up in foster care until ultimately reunited with their father. This powerful novel glimpses the political process, the difficulties of a new school, and the refugee experience through a child's eyes.

## Sitti's Secrets
BY NAOMI SHIHAB NYE
ILLUSTRATED BY NANCY CARPENTER
ALADDIN, 1997. (I)

In America, Mona recalls visiting her *sitti*, her Palestinian grandmother. While neither speaks the other's language, they share happy experiences, communicate by gesture and love, and use Mona's father as a go-between and translator. The book invites talk about distant relatives, special relationships with older people, and the challenges of being bicultural.

## Snake Charmer
BY ANN WHITEHEAD NAGDA
HENRY HOLT, 2002. (I)

Vibrant photographs show how a snake charmer near Agra, India, makes his living by removing holy snakes from people's homes and entertaining in the city with a cobra in a basket. The children, Vishnu and his sisters, study hard so they will have a better job. A good addition to an exploration of jobs around the world, the book also brings the reader closer to issues and life in developing areas of the world.

## Under the Mango Tree
BY AMY BRONWEN ZEMSER
GREENWILLOW, 1998. (U)

Sarina is a 12-year-old American girl living in Liberia, caring for her mother whose erratic behavior goes beyond her diabetes. The girl's only companions are the servants, until she meets a young African boy, Boima, who broadens her world by sharing his loving family and traditional stories from his culture. The contrast between the cultures within one country, expectations, and living what you've learned are explored here in the gripping though sometimes uncomfortable portrait of Liberia painted in Sarina's voice.

## Vejigante Masquerader
### BY LULU DELACRE
SCHOLASTIC, 1993. (P, I)

In this bilingual story, Ramón resourcefully manages to get a costume together for the Puerto Rican celebration of Carnival. He seeks help from the best seamstress in town, works for the mask-maker to buy his papier mâché mask, and joins the bigger boys. When a goat ruins his costume, his mother steps in and together they repair the damage. This is an introduction to one of the many festival types found throughout Latin America and good story for talking about persistence and working for what you want. Directions for making a mask are included, too.

## Voices: Poetry and Art from Around the World
### SELECTED BY BARBARA BRENNER
ILLUSTRATED WITH PHOTOGRAPHS
NATIONAL GEOGRAPHIC, 2000. (I, U)

Poetry from six continents is paired with clear reproductions of art, artifacts, and photographs. Poets and the forms they use are as varied as the striking visuals used to create a sense of the hugeness of our world and some of the commonalities among its inhabitants.

# Chapter 6

# looking IN A Mirror

It's a lifelong task to discover who you are and what you believe. And it can be a scary task, too. Finding out who you are involves taking risks, reaching out to others, accepting or seeking help, and learning from mistakes. Although growth is inevitable, most of us alternately crave and fear change and the self-knowledge it can bring.

Children, like adults, seek evidence they are growing. They shoulder up to classmates to see who's tallest. They scamper onto scales at the doctor's office to see how much they've gained. They wriggle with delight when last summer's sandals no longer fit. They want to know their efforts to grow are working.

Perhaps that's one of the reasons kids like sports. Turning that first double play across first base, popping an ollie on a skateboard, or plunging off the high dive are hard-won evidence of "getting better." One of the roles of parents, teachers, mentors, and other adults is to offer encouragement, to say—"Look how you've grown!" or "Look what you can do now that you couldn't do as well last time!"

Learning to deal with feelings is a challenging part of growing up. Children need practice in dealing with emotions and talking about them beyond the preschooler's limited "mad" or "sad." Frustration, anxiety, fear, nervousness, reluctance, shyness, or remorse are complicated sorts of feelings. Books that provide children with an emotional vocabulary—whose messages are straightforward and purposeful—are invaluable in helping children scale life's hilly terrain. From Saxton Freymann's whimsical *How Are You Peeling?* to the more solemn, *Mick Harte Was Here* by Barbara Park, great books show that growth comes when we can talk about our feelings rather than merely act on or ignore them.

## Growing **Pains**

As your children grow, you don't get the opportunity to have those warm and fuzzy bedtime stories anymore. As my son moved into his teen years, we evolved from the "snuggle and cuddle" stage to talking about articles from *U.S. News and World Report* or *Sports Illustrated* and occasional discussions about what he was reading in school. I missed connecting with him through books. Then one day we read the same book independently and rushed to tell each other what we thought about it. I began to see my son shine; he was stretching to empathize and to experience difficult situations through the safety net of a book. If more parents took this approach, children might be more comfortable talking to us about their "growing pains."

Books in this chapter feature characters who change, become a bit more firmly themselves, or grow up a little. Often these young characters accomplish something they didn't think they could pull off, as does the reluctant rodent in *Little Rat Sets Sail* by Monica Bang-Campbell. Some go against adult expectations, while others reach a compromise. In books intended for older readers, the adults often change their minds and give a child more respect. This happens to Cara Landry, the fifth-grade news reporter in Andrew Clement's *The Landry News*, when her teacher tells her that she's made a real difference in his life.

Sometimes adults in these stories, such as Nathan's father in *Storm Warriors* by Elisa Carbone, serve as mentors to help the child at the story's center. It's similar in real life to the parent, librarian, teacher, or other grownup who, by inspiring readers to talk about these book characters and their choices, help children make the connections to their own lives.

All growing things need nurturing, and children need to know that their budding talents and interests are important. Biographies not only show how people grow up; these wonderful life stories show how persistent interests can lead to adult careers, contributions to society, and personal fulfillment. A childhood interest in art and storytelling enabled Tomie de Paola and

Helen Lester to grow into beloved picture book creators. In Jacqueline Martin's *Snowflake Bentley*, a boy photographed snowflakes and laid the foundation for the science of microphotography. In Michelle Green's *A Strong Right Arm: The Story of Mamie "Peanut" Johnson*, a girl's love of baseball enabled her to become the only woman to pitch professionally on a men's team. Biographies inspire young readers to dream. They also allow young readers to vicariously experience little moments of growing. When the character in the story acts with courage or generosity, makes choices or hard decisions, and learns from mistakes, he or she models thoughtful action to the child reader.

By following the lives of the characters, real and fictional, readers will be introduced to a wide range of human possibility. Discussed thoughtfully, these books will help children feel more secure about that person they see in the mirror every morning and more excited about the person they'll become.

## CHRIS SOENTPIET *is an illustrator whose lush images and colors transport the reader into different lives and cultures. He often uses real models for his moving books, such as* **More Than Anything Else** *and* **Something Beautiful**.

**This is a nation of diverse cultures, both immigrant and native. How important is it for kids to see themselves in the books they read?**

Very important. Kids need to know where they came from because they can learn and draw power from their history and their family's past. All of these experiences enrich us. Children who read should have the experience of finding themselves in the characters they read about, through their expressions and discoveries and even dreams. Real people anchor the illustrations and the story. That's what makes a good book.

# RECOMMENDED Books

P = PRIMARY (KINDERGARTEN – GRADE 3)
I = INTERMEDIATE (GRADE 3 – GRADE 4)
U = UPPER (GRADE 4 – GRADE 6)

## America's Champion Swimmer: Gertrude Ederle

BY DAVID ADLER
ILLUSTRATED BY TERRY WIDENER
GULLIVER, 2000. (P, I)

By the time she was 19, Gertrude Ederle had set numerous records and, in the 1920s, became the first woman to swim the English Channel. But Trudy wasn't born a swimmer. In fact, she nearly drowned when she was seven and so was taught by her father to dog paddle. With courage, Trudy went on to perfect her skills, overcome coaching sexism, set Olympic records, swim the Channel, and become a world-class athlete. This picture book biography shows how a determined woman athlete paved the way for other female athletes, and illustrator Widener's sturdy depiction of the characters is well-suited to the subject.

## Anastasia Krupnik

BY LOIS LOWRY
HOUGHTON MIFFLIN, 1979. (U)

Anastasia keeps a list of "Things I love" and "Things I hate" but throughout the book, as she waits for the birth of her new brother, the things on the list keep switching categories. This story offers children good insights into the nature of changing opinions as new experiences provoke new thoughts for Anastasia. This book about

Anastasia and Phyllis Reynolds Naylor's *The Agony of Alice* (Atheneum, 1985) introduce two popular series that depict girls growing from middle elementary school into middle school. (Series)

## Angel Spreads Her Wings

BY JUDY DELTON
HOUGHTON MIFFLIN, 1999. (I)

Angel and her family are headed to Greece to meet the new grandparents and relatives that come with her mother's remarriage. A first-class worrier, Angel hates changes and thinks of all the things that can go wrong. Indeed some do, but Angel discovers she likes her new family, feels a little bit braver, and is enriched by her newfound Greek cultural connections. Other books in the series also feature moments of growing up and adults who help. (Series)

## Arthur for the Very First Time

BY PATRICIA MACLACHLAN
ILLUSTRATED BY LLOYD BLOOM
HARPERCOLLINS, 1980. (I, U)

Sent away to his eccentric relatives' farm because his mother is having a difficult pregnancy, Arthur takes refuge in writing in his journal. When Arthur hides in introspection, his exuberant new friend Moira calls him "Mouse" until finally Arthur takes a chance and shows what he can do. Then Moira calls Arthur by his name—for the very first time. This story about coming out of one's shell and taking risks is full of talking points about courage plus accepting differences. Pay particular attention to what the italicized words indicate.

### The Art Lesson

BY TOMIE DE PAOLA
PUTNAM, 1989. (P)

In one of his many autobiographical picture books, de Paola tells of Tommie, a boy who loves to draw. While his parents and family encourage him, the art teachers at school insist on prescribed lessons and coloring inside the lines. Finally, one teacher allows him just to draw. The book will trigger discussion about what experiences nurture talent and the ways adults can help; it also has a strong message about persevering. Other autobiographical de Paola books that celebrate being oneself include *Oliver Button is a Sissy* (Harcourt, 1979), *26 Fairmont Street* (see Chapter 1), and *Tom* (Putnam, 1993). These provide a fine introduction to an author/illustrator who is one of the most prolific creators of American children's books.

### Author: A True Story

BY HELEN LESTER
HOUGHTON MIFFLIN, 1997. (P, I)

Though she knew by age three that she wanted to be a writer, Helen Lester (author of, among other books, *Tacky the Penguin*, Houghton, 1988) had to persevere to overcome the frustrations of writing in school. She had trouble recognizing the difference between the letters *b* and *d*, veered into mirror writing, and struggled with organization. Later, as an adult, she had to learn to tolerate rejections of her books before one was accepted for publication. Still she kept faith in herself: "I was the first author I had ever met." Her self-illustrated autobiography is funny, poignant, revealing, encouraging, and sure to inspire readers and, of course, writers.

### The Bat Boy and the Violin

BY GAVIN CURTIS
ILLUSTRATED BY E.B. LEWIS
SIMON & SCHUSTER, 1998. (P, I)

In this story of parent and child conflict over what is important, Papa is coach of "the worst baseball team in the Negro League" and Reginald loves to play his violin. But Papa needs a bat boy. The two resolve this conflict with surprising results for the team. This is a good book for talking about disagreements with a parent, hobbies that can become important, and the old Negro League era. Lensey Namioka's novel for older children, *Yang the Youngest and His Terrible Ear* (Chapter 1), is based on two of these themes.

### Bud, Not Buddy

BY CHRISTOPHER PAUL CURTIS
DELACORTE, 1999. (U)

Orphaned at six, Bud runs away from a string of bad foster homes looking for the man he believes to be his father. Bud's sometimes laugh-out-loud funny journey, told in his naive voice, is filled with survival tips, drama, information about the African-American traveling bands in the 1930s, and the memorable people he meets. The difference between what Bud finds on his journey compared with what he originally sought should ignite discussion, as will the dilemmas of the poor in Depression-era Michigan. Note, too, the fascinating afterword in which Curtis shows how his research and his own family history inform this fictional story.

### Chang and the Bamboo Flute

BY ELIZABETH STARR HILL
ILLUSTRATED BY LESLEY LIU
FARRAR, STRAUS & GIROUX, 2002. (I)

When a flood damages their houseboat, Chang and his family must find shelter in a barn belonging to his friend, Mei Mei. Chang, who can't speak, is shy about playing his treasured flute and wants to keep his talents private. But he makes a courageous decision when his family needs his support. Chang and Mei Mei were introduced in *Bird Boy* (Farrar, Straus & Giroux, 1999).

### Crispin: The Cross of Lead

BY AVI
HYPERION, 2002. (U)

In 14th-century England, a boy named Crispin escapes a treacherous feudal lord after the death of his mother. An illiterate, Crispin is declared a "wolf's head"—wanted dead or alive. His only possession is a lead cross that holds the secret to his real identity. When Crispin meets a huge man named Bear, they develop a close, though unlikely, friendship. Bear helps Crispin learn that he is the illegitimate son of the manor lord. Narrative twists and turns create a tense, fast-paced novel that can begin a discussion of medieval life, how an individual finds his or her own identity, and how friendship changes both Crispin and Bear.

## Dream Carver

BY DIANA COHN
ILLUSTRATED BY AMY CÓRDOVA
CHRONICLE BOOKS, 2002. (I)

Like his father, Manuel carves *jugetes*, tiny wooden animals, in the marketplace. He dreams of carving larger, more brightly colored animals but his father disapproves. So in secret, Manuel produces a new kind of carving, one the villagers love, which sparks the renaissance of Mexican woodcarving. The story, inspired by the life of Oaxacan carver Manuel Jimenez, is illustrated with conventions borrowed from Mexican folk art. An endnote in this picture book explains the story's nonfiction underpinnings. Readers can talk about where artists get their ideas, how people feel when someone thinks of a new way of doing something, and the importance of art in our lives.

## Eleanor Roosevelt: A Life of Discovery

BY RUSSELL FREEDMAN
HOUGHTON MIFFLIN, 1997. (U)

In spite of her childhood, Eleanor, a shy child from a privileged but dysfunctional family, grew into a courageous, far-thinking, accomplished woman. Beyond being the wife of President Franklin Delano Roosevelt, Eleanor's own accomplishments are documented in this well-written biography. A sense of Eleanor's independence and self-assuredness is found in a book for younger readers, *Amelia and Eleanor Go for a Ride: Based on a True Story* by Pam Muñoz Ryan, illustrated by Brian Selznick (Scholastic, 1999). In it, Eleanor Roosevelt and aviator Amelia Earhart leave a White House dinner for a little spin in Amelia's plane.

## Ella Fitzgerald: The Tale of a Vocal Virtuoso

BY ANDREA PINKNEY
ILLUSTRATED BY BRIAN PINKNEY
HYPERION, 2002. (P, I)

Readers follow the growth and impact of jazz great Ella Fitzgerald in rhythmic text and swirling, tinted scratchboard illustrations. This story is told by a lively "hepcat" named Scat Cat Monroe in four "tracks," or chapters. Not only is the creative life of this gifted singer worth discussing, so is the way the Pinkneys present her story in language and artwork. Interested readers might listen to Ella's singing, look further into the roots of jazz and the time in which Ella lived, and get to know some of her musical contemporaries. *Duke Ellington: The Piano Prince and His Orchestra* (Hyperion, 1998) is by the same husband and wife team.

## Feather Boy

BY NICK SINGER
DELACORTE, 2002. (U)

Twelve-year-old Robert Nobel just doesn't fit in; he's awkward and gangly, the butt of school jokes and bullying. While participating in an art project with a group of older people, Robert meets Edith, an elderly woman with stories and a painful past. This friendship allows Robert to confront his greatest fears. He learns he can control who he is becoming, and the meaning of flying, a metaphor for the lightness of spirit he feels. The subplots of this intriguing British novel all come together as each character grows and changes.

## Frida

BY JONAH WINTER
ILLUSTRATED BY ANA JUAN
SCHOLASTIC/ARTHUR A. LEVINE, 2002. (I)

Rich paintings in the style of Mexican folk art illustrate this brief and moving glimpse of Frida Kahlo. This story of a Mexican-born woman who overcame suffering to become a gifted artist combines a simple yet powerful text with illustrations featuring symbols she used in her own work. Winter's *Diego* (Knopf, 1994), illustrated by his mother Jeanette Winter, is a picture book biography of Frida Kahlo's husband, Diego Rivera.

## The Gardener

BY SARAH STEWART
ILLUSTRATED BY DAVID SMALL
FARRAR, STRAUS & GIROUX, 1997. (I)

Sent to the city to live with an undemonstrative uncle because her family has fallen on financial hard times, Lydia gradually transforms the drab bakery and apartment where her uncle spends his time. The Depression-era story is told in letters that enable readers to deduce changes in Lydia even as she changes her uncle and his city spaces. Readers might also talk about gardening as a metaphor for the growth of both characters.

## Henry and Mudge and the Happy Cat

BY CYNTHIA RYLANT
ILLUSTRATED BY SUÇIE STEVENSON
BRADBURY PRESS, 1990. (P)

Henry brings home a "shabby" stray cat that he and his dog Mudge quickly come to love and want to keep. Soon, the cat is mothering the huge dog and endearing itself to the family. But Mother notes they don't need another pet because "taking care of Mudge is like taking care of five dogs." So they advertise the rescued cat and its owner, a police officer, comes to claim it. The sadness Henry and Mudge feel is eased by hugs and a nap. Not only that, the cat's owner leaves behind a box of big dog bones and a police badge, which Mudge generously shares with his boy. In the many realistic books about these two friends, repetition of a few challenging words and three short chapters give new readers support. Stories threaded with gentle humor encourage children to talk about their own similar experiences. (Series)

## Jason Rat-a-Tat

BY COLBY RODOWSKY
ILLUSTRATED BY BETH PECK
FARRAR, STRAUS & GIROUX, 2002. (I)

Jason spends plenty of time fooling around in and under the bleachers while his older sister and brother follow their hectic schedule of games and practices. While his family tries to encourage him to take up a sport, it's his grandfather who notices Jason drumming on things and gives him sticks, a drum, and lessons. Jason's tale is a good starting point for talking about family dynamics, the enormous potential that lies in exploring your own interests, and ways people discover and nurture talent.

## Journey to an 800 Number

BY E.L. KONIGSBURG
ATHENEUM, 1982. (U)

From his wealthy stepfather, preppy Bo has adopted snobbish ways. When he reluctantly visits his father, who works as a camel keeper for the circus, Bo meets plenty of characters who are not what he expected, but who all love his father. Then Bo has to rethink his prejudices, his views on what's truly important, and his feelings about his father and himself. This often funny book shows how, if given some time in new situations, people can come to change their minds and grow up a little.

## The Landry News

BY ANDREW CLEMENT
SIMON & SCHUSTER, 1999. (U)

Fifth grader Cara Landry starts a class newspaper and in it she points out that her disillusioned teacher Mr. Larson isn't teaching them. Although threatened with dismissal by the principal, Mr. Larson begins to change and the class comes to care about him and what they're learning. This humorous but thoughtful book offers many jumping off points for a great discussion, including what makes a good teacher, why people change, whether 10-year-olds have First Amendment rights, and what comprises good journalism.

## Little Rat Sets Sail

BY MONICA BANG-CAMPBELL
ILLUSTRATED BY MOLLY BANG
HARCOURT, 2002. (P, I)

Little Rat is nervous about learning to sail, especially when she begins to think about the big ocean and what's hidden beneath the waves. But during a summer of trying new things, like hoisting the sail and keeping her spirits up through a sudden squall, Little Rat discovers a little bit of courage she didn't know she had. Young children can discuss how Little Rat's character blossoms as she triumphs over one challenge after another. Readers will also have fun hunting for the sailing terms cleverly incorporated into the pictures, diagrams, and text of this easy-reader story.

## Max

BY BOB GRAHAM
CANDLEWICK, 2000. (P)

As the child of two super-parents, you'd think Max would fly right away. But as much as he tries, he just can't manage, much to his schoolmates' and family's consternation. Then, Max sees a baby bird that needs rescuing and suddenly he's aloft. A good discussion point is posed by Max's friend when he says "Everyone's different in *some* way." This oversized picture book, with cheerful cartoon-like illustrations, opens discussion about doing something when you're ready, a theme of Robert Kraus' *Leo the Late Bloomer* (illustrated by José Aruego and Ariane Dewey, Crowell, 1971).

## Mick Harte Was Here

BY BARBARA PARK
APPLE SOUP, 1995. (U)

Phoebe narrates the story of her younger brother who died in a bicycle accident. Devastated, the family grieves with an enormous number of "if onlys." Finally, they compile a list of these regrets as a way to stop blaming themselves and go forward. Park includes an afterword about bicycle safety, a subject most older readers can discuss from personal experience. Like *Fig Pudding* by Ralph Fletcher, in Chapter 1, this book helps readers talk about how a family changes as it deals with death.

## Not My Dog

BY COLBY RODOWSKY
ILLUSTRATED BY THOMAS F. YEZERSKI
FARRAR, STRAUS & GIROUX, 1999. (I)

Ellie is about to get a promised puppy when she turns nine but instead has to settle for a hand-me-down dog because her great-aunt is moving to an assisted living apartment and can't have pets. Readers will want to talk about Ellie's decision, parental "advice," and whether she did the right thing. They'll also enjoy looking at the end of each chapter to note how the author lets us in on Ellie's gradual change of mind.

## Ramona Quimby, Age 8

BY BEVERLY CLEARY
ILLUSTRATED BY ALAN TIEGREEN
MORROW, 1981. (I)

This later book in the series about the irrepressible Ramona features the many adjustments she makes to accommodate her mother's full-time work and her father's new role as an art student. Ramona rides the bus, stays with old Mrs. Kemp until her parents come home, and tackles third grade. Children will respond to the way Ramona adapts to so many changes, the realistic depiction of eight-year-olds in a school setting, and the gentle humor of the telling, even as the book deals with serious themes. (Series)

## The Real, True Dulcie Campbell

BY CYNTHIA DEFELICE
ILLUSTRATED BY R.W. ALLEY
FARRAR, STRAUS & GIROUX, 2002. (P)

Dulcie Campbell thinks that she really must be a princess, not the daughter of farmers with muck on their boots. But when Dulcie realizes that only a fairy tale princess would have to deal with the ogres and other creatures she imagines in the darkening barn, she comes to appreciate being herself. This fancifully illustrated tale explores the desire to try on another identity and the ultimate satisfaction in accepting yourself.

## Rocks in His Head

BY CAROL OTIS HURST
ILLUSTRATED BY JAMES STEVENSON
GREENWILLOW, 2001. (I)

This affectionate fictionalized picture book biography of the author's father introduces readers to a man who loved rocks and geology. In spite of a national economic depression and world war, his father is able to find a job as a janitor in a natural history museum. Ultimately, he ends up as the curator of rocks and his passion became his vocation. The story invites children to note how a character pursued his interests and to reflect on qualities and interests they have now that might grow into some occupation or hobby later.

## The Rough-Face Girl

BY RAFE MARTIN
ILLUSTRATED BY DAVID SHANNON
PUTNAM'S, 1992. (P, I)

In the Algonquin version of "Cinderella," the Rough-Face girl has faith in herself despite her poor appearance, and through her courage and own perseverance, becomes the bride of the Invisible Being. As a metaphor for believing in yourself, this folktale has no equal. While it stands on its own, it's also a good basis for comparing the many non-European "Cinderella" variants currently available. For another take on the the Cinderella story, see Ellen Jackson's *Cinder Edna* in Chapter 7.

## Ruby Holler

BY SHARON CREECH
JOANNA COTLER/HARPERCOLLINS, 2002. (U)

Dallas and Florida, the "trouble twins," are living in a dreadful Dickensian orphanage after being tossed from one foster home to another. Luckily, they are sent to live with the elderly Sairy and Tiller in rural Ruby Holler. Suspicious at first, the twins gradually respond to Sairy's patience and good cooking, backed up by head-clearing doses of the outdoors. Along the way, they gain hope, trust, and a family. Betsy Byars' often-humorous *Pinballs* (HarperCollins, 1977) is a slightly less dramatic but equally gripping story about three foster children changing their lives a bit at a time. Katherine Paterson picks up the theme in *The Great Gilly Hopkins* (Crowell, 1978), a book in which challenging writing and a bittersweet ending pose terrific discussions for older readers. Taken together, these three books about the struggles of finding family ask readers to consider whether the characters made the right decisions and what the futures might hold for them after the book ends.

## Snowflake Bentley

BY JACQUELINE BRIGGS MARTIN
ILLUSTRATED BY MARY AZARIAN
HOUGHTON MIFFLIN, 1998. (I, U)

Stunning tinted woodcuts seem the perfect medium to tell the story of the boy in the late 1800s who saw the world close-up. With an old microscope from his mother, the Vermont boy looked at grass, raindrops, flowers, and snowflakes. His passion for drawing snowflakes led to experimentation with cold-weather photography, and finally the now-common technique of microphotography. Central text framed by informational sidebars offer two ways to read this picture book biography about Wilson Bentley.

## Staying Nine

BY PAM CONRAD
ILLUSTRATED BY MIKE WIMMER
HARPERCOLLINS, 1990. (I)

Heather is nervous about aging into double digits, so her mother helps her plan an un-birthday party. But it's her uncle's girlfriend who helps Heather see that growing up isn't a bad thing at all. Jannell Cannon's *Verdi* (Harcourt, 1997) presents the same theme but for younger children, and Madeleine L'Engle's challenging classic, *A Wind in the Door* (Farrar, Straus & Giroux, 1973), suggests what might happen to the world if some small part of nature decided not to grow up.

## Storm Warriors

BY ELISA CARBONE
KNOPF, 2001. (U)

In 1895, Nathan, his father, and grandfather, a former slave, move to Pea Island on North Carolina's Outer Banks. Working as a fisherman, Nathan is inspired by the courage and excitement shown by the African-American crew of the U.S. life-saving station. But the Coast Guard suddenly transfers all Black surfmen to this single station and there's no room for an apprentice. Still, Nathan sneaks aboard a rescue mission and nearly drowns. Ultimately, he realizes that he can channel his desire to save lives in other directions and winds up in the field of medicine. Nathan is fictitious, but this exciting novel is based on actual post-Civil War events.

## A Strong Right Arm: The Story of Mamie "Peanut" Johnson

BY MICHELLE Y. GREEN
DIAL, 2002. (I, U)

Mamie Johnson loved baseball. In spite of all obstacles, this woman, nicknamed for her 5'2" height, played professional baseball for the Negro Leagues' Indianapolis Clowns as a pitcher, learning the curve ball from Satchel Paige. This intimate glimpse of an extraordinary person, one of only three women to play in the Negro Leagues, should spark children to talk about the results of her perseverance and passion, as well as baseball's place in the history of the United States.

## Today I Feel Silly and Other Moods that Make My Day

BY JAMIE LEE CURTIS
ILLUSTRATED BY LAURA CORNELL
HARPERCOLLINS, 1998 (P)

This popular book lists in rhyme the many moods a cheerful and energetic girl may experience in one day. It's a reassuring catalogue of typical things that give joy, such as pancakes and racing around, as well as things that are hard to take, like being left out of a play date or falling on your roller blades. Readers will want to chronicle their own moods or draw self-portraits and describe their feelings. Saxton Freymann's creative manipulation of fruit and vegetables in *How Are You Peeling?* (Scholastic, 1999) also helps children develop an emotional vocabulary.

## What Charlie Heard
BY MORDECAI GERSTEIN
FRANCES FOSTER BOOKS, 2002. (I)

Composer Charles Ives was "born with his ears wide open," according to this lively picture book biography. The illustrator shows readers what Ives hears with overlaid renditions of sound effect words (lines of *clangs*, explosions of *booms*), exuberant color, and other design elements that show how the natural world enhanced Ives' exploration of what percussive music could be. This book provides a great introduction to a prominent 20th-century composer and it begs children to listen to Ives' music. It also raises the question about where artists, songwriters, or musicians get their ideas.

## When Marian Sang
BY PAM MUÑOZ RYAN
ILLUSTRATED BY BRIAN SELZNICK
SCHOLASTIC, 2002. (I, U)

Presented theatrically as if staged for our enjoyment, this touching picture book biography of Marian Anderson depicts the life of one of the most revered singers in America. Sepia illustrations reflect Anderson's modesty and inward-looking performances (she often sang with her eyes closed), while the words tell how she remained true to her talent while rising above racial prejudice in the 1930s to become one of the symbols of the Civil Rights movement. Don't miss the two end notes, which tell how author and illustrator were drawn into their research by personal connections.

## When Sophie Gets Angry—Really, Really Angry
BY MOLLY BANG
SCHOLASTIC, 1999. (P)

Sophie explains what she does when anger wells up and clouds her thinking. Learning how to control your emotions and behaviors without adult intervention is a sign of growth, and the book's vibrant illustrations use color and brush strokes to convey this progression. Ask readers to swap useful strategies they and their families use, or could use, to channel and control anger or impulsive behaviors. Another book about anger management is Rachel Vail's wise *Sometimes I'm Bombaloo*, illustrated by Yumi Heo (Scholastic, 2002).

## Where I'd Like To Be
BY FRANCES O'ROARK DOWELL
ATHENEUM, 2003. (U)

According to her grandmother, Maddie is special—she was saved by ghosts as a baby. But now that her grandmother can no longer take care of her, the sixth grader is living at the East Tennessee Children's Home and, except in the eyes of six-year-old Ricky Ray, is not very special at all. To comfort herself, Maddie cuts pictures from magazines and creates a Book of Houses and a Book of People, which she shares with the charismatic new girl, Murphy. Together, they form a club and build a hut, or "real home," in the woods. Maddie begins to open up—until someone ruins her scrapbooks. Well-drawn diverse characters, a believable setting, and strong descriptions, plus a hopeful future for Maddie will spur discussion about friendships, the power of homeplaces, and how losses challenge us to grow stronger.

## Wilma Unlimited: How Wilma Rudolph Became the World's Fastest Woman
BY KATHERINE KRULL
ILLUSTRATED BY DAVID DIAZ
HARCOURT, 1996. (P, I)

Wilma Rudolph was the first woman to win three gold medals in a single Olympics. Her tenacity, courage, and character allowed her to overcome potentially devastating obstacles: partial paralysis from polio as a young child, choosing to compete in a man's sport, and growing up African American in the segregated South of the 1940s. Her story is told in highly stylized illustrations and a straightforward, and affecting, text that will generate discussion and inspire children to learn more about Wilma and the times in which she lived.

# Chapter 7

# Laughing Together

A snicker, a sniggle, a full-fledged guffaw. What makes us laugh? Cows that can type? The antics of a surprise birthday chicken? Trying to say "baby in a bubble" three times fast?

Children laugh at all sorts of things as they develop a sense of humor. How that sense of humor develops depends on a child's intellectual and emotional growth. In his book *What's So Funny?*, Michael Cart identifies 10 categories or types of humor (HarperCollins, 1995). Among them are exaggeration, incongruity, surprise, slapstick, and the absurd, which includes nonsense and silliness. With such tasty dishes on the comic buffet, it's easy to see why elementary age children find the demanding cows in Betsy Lewin's *Click, Clack, Moo: Cows That Type* or the wisecracking "ductective" in Margie Palatini's *The Web Files* so appealing.

Children in the middle elementary grades appreciate the humor of human predicaments—like Alex in *Skinnybones* by Barbara Park, who is caught by his mother in an elaborate lie about spilled cat food. Children also appreciate being "in on the joke," hence the popularity of the well-intentioned maid in Peggy Parrish's *Amelia Bedelia*, who interprets dressing a fowl literally, and an exploring chicken in Janet Stoeke's *Minerva Louise*, who mistakes school cubbies for nest boxes. The reader knows all along what the main character is about to discover and can revel in the anticipation of what will happen next. Jokes (especially knock-knock jokes) and riddles put the teller in charge because he or she already knows the answers, another form of being in on the joke.

Laughing together builds a wonderful community spirit. Laughing has no curriculum—it doesn't appear on anyone's list of essential standards of learn-

## I'm a Nonsense!

Living in the adult world with looming deadlines and hectic schedules, we sometimes forget how to laugh. That's why I look forward to seeing Glenda, my young reading buddy. One day Glenda couldn't pronounce the word "nuisance." So, I said it for her. A little unsure, she frowned a bit. "What does nuisance mean?" she asked. "It means someone's a 'pain,'" I told her. "Oh YES!" she said proudly, a huge smile lighting up her face, "I'm a nuisance. Just ask my mom!" Later, as we were leaving, she shouted excitedly to her friend, "Guess what? My reading buddy says I'm a nonsense!"

CHRISTINE HANNIS
READING BUDDIES PROGRAM
WASHINGTON, D.C.

ing. In fact, parents and teachers often underestimate the power of laughter. But books that provoke a cheery chuckle or an all-out belly laugh invite children to delight in language, release tension, diffuse anger, share others' predicaments, solve problems, and take joy in being together. Even though what's considered funny in one part of the world may not be what tickles people's fancies somewhere else, laughter itself is a universal expression. Whether telling stories about popping down a rabbit hole in Victorian England or dancing with crows on the Zuni plains, humorous books reinforce the idea that laughter is a language spoken everywhere.

All children enjoy verbal humor, but it takes a certain amount of sophistication to appreciate the puns, allusions, and funny asides that many stories include. To engage young readers, there's a plethora of word play in poetry and abundant amusement in alliteration, and who can resist the sumptuous sounds storytellers select to spice up folktales? Words themselves can be funny. Imagine the fun of reading "noodlehead" stories from around the world, trying to pronounce the cobbled-together words in Roald Dahl's *The BFG*, or meeting such over-the-top characters as Dav Pilkey's *Dogzilla* or Russell Hoban's Aunt Fidget Wonkham-Strong in *How Tom Beat Captain Najork and his Hired Sportsmen*.

There's a cruel side to children's humor as well; ridicule, defiance, and violence elicit nervous laughter. Fittingly, we seldom find this type of humor in books for elementary age children, prevalent though it may be on the playground, in the neighborhood, and in the verbal sparring between kids that adults may not witness.

Many children don't know when to laugh. Haven't you seen kids wondering, with earnest faces, "Is it okay to laugh now? Can I laugh out loud, or will that get me in trouble with the grownups?" Go ahead, hand out wholesale permission! The books on this list offer plenty of opportunities to set off fits of giggling among your favorite children—then you can invite them to let you in on the joke. And isn't that what it's all about? Laughter is even better when it's shared.

**PAMELA EDWARDS** *AND* **HENRY COLE** *are an author and illustrator duo joined at the funny bone. Their books—comical, often alliterative texts with humorous illustrations to match—are popular with readers, young and old. Together, they've created many books including* **Warthogs in a Box** *and* **Dinorella***.*

**Many of your books play with words and images. Why do you think yours and other humorous books can be used in the classroom?**

As former teachers, both of us can tell you there's nothing like humor to carry a lesson. Children remember facts that are presented humorously rather than those delivered in a dry, dull manner. Both of us learned to teach early on with a great sense of humor and that has found its way to our books as well.

# RECOMMENDED Books

P = PRIMARY (KINDERGARTEN – GRADE 3)
I = INTERMEDIATE (GRADE 3 – GRADE 4)
U = UPPER (GRADE 4 – GRADE 6)

## Alice's Adventures in Wonderland

**BY LEWIS CARROLL**
VARIOUS ILLUSTRATORS, COMPILED BY COOPER EDENS
CHRONICLE BOOKS, 2000. (I, U)

This classic tale of the child who fell down a rabbit
hole is full of wordplay, ludicrous situations,
exaggerated characters, and funny scenes. Edens
punctuates Carroll's text with pictures selected
from illustrated versions from the last 100 years.
The story was originally illustrated by John Tenniel,
but other illustrators, such as Lisbeth Zwerger,
Abelard Morell, Helen Oxenbury, and Angel
Dominguez have created their own visual world
from Carroll's words. Just looking at versions
by different illustrators helps children appreciate
the way artists subtly interpret the story.

## All of Our Noses Are Here and Other Noodle Tales

**BY ALVIN SCHWARTZ**
ILLUSTRATED BY KAREN ANN WEINHAUS
HARPERCOLLINS, 1985. (I)

The Browns are the really silly family first introduced in *There's a Carrot in My Ear and Other
Noodle Tales* (HarperCollins, 1982). These absurd
stories with broad humor, retold here to be acces-
sible to newly independent readers, are based on
traditional folktales—also known as noodlehead
stories—from around the world.

## The BFG

**BY ROALD DAHL**
ILLUSTRATED BY QUENTIN BLAKE
FARRAR, STRAUS & GIROUX, 1982. (I, U)

This is one of the most beloved and least ornery
of Dahl's books, which tells of Sophie's encounter
with a huge giant who bestows dreams on children.
Dahl's wordplay includes funny giant names,
plenty of made-up words, tongue twisters, and
ludicrous situations in which Sophie finds herself.
Children will have a hilarious time translating
their own stories into Dahl-speak and then
reading aloud to each other.

## Bubble Trouble and Other Poems and Stories

**BY MARGARET MAHY**
McELDERRY, 1992. (I, U)

The title poem sets the tone for this appealing,
thin volume. It uses tongue-twisting alliteration,
rhyme, and wordplay to reveal the trouble with
errant bubbles. The poem makes a good read
aloud and is sure to cause laughs for both readers
(try saying "baby in a bubble" quickly!) and
listeners.

## Burnt Toast on Davenport Street

**BY TIM EGAN**
HOUGHTON MIFFLIN, 1997. (P)

Arthur and Stella, a dog couple, have "a nice life.
Not perfect, but nice" in a cozy bungalow, except
for a gang of rowdy and rude crocodiles who hang
out on the corner. When Arthur thinks he's humor-
ing a fly spared from the swatter, he doesn't take
the wishes the fly has granted very seriously—

until they come true! Understated language combines with deadpan illustrations to tell an outlandish and very funny story.

## Cinder Edna

BY ELLEN JACKSON
ILLUSTRATED BY KEVIN O'MALLEY
LOTHROP, 1994. (I)

This well-known tale has been retold to contrast sisters: Cinder Ella's passivity to Cinder Edna's spunk and independence. Humor in both text and illustration will generate giggles and perhaps discussion about different outlooks and approaches to life. Frances Minters' *Cinder-Elly* (illustrated by G. Brian Karas, Viking, 1994) makes the tale a rhyming urban rap, Babette Cole retells it with a male hero in *Prince Cinders* (Putnam, 1997), and *Cindy Ellen: A Wild Western Cinderella* by Susan Lowell (illustrated by Jane Manning, HarperCollins, 2000) rounds out a study of funny takeoffs on the familiar tale.

## Click, Clack, Moo: Cows That Type

BY DOREEN CRONIN
ILLUSTRATED BY BETSY LEWIN
SIMON & SCHUSTER, 2000. (P)

The pure silliness of cows who type is offset by what they type—demands for electric blankets to stay warm in the barn. When the farmer won't meet their demands, the cows go on strike ("No milk today") and they send Duck to mediate. The twist at the end provokes even more giggles. In fact, the next book is called *Giggle, Giggle, Quack* (Simon & Schuster, 2002) and Farmer Brown goes on vacation. Big mistake.

## "Could Be Worse!"

BY JAMES STEVENSON
MORROW, 1977. (P)

It's boring at Grandpa's until the day he spins a yarn for his two grandchildren and takes them on an adventure filled with exaggeration and laugh-out-loud happenings. Stevenson's cartoon-like illustrations perfectly complement his understated humor in this and many others of his books. Note the many hand-lettered types of print and the way Stevenson shows energy and movement. (Series)

## Coyote: A Trickster Tale from the American Southwest

BY GERALD MCDERMOTT
HARCOURT BRACE, 1994. (P, I)

In this Zuni Pueblo tale, foolish Coyote is just too eager to join the orderly line of chanting, dancing, and flying crows. So Old Man Crow tricks the trickster in a humorous story of trying to be what you are not. McDermott's illustrations, using stunning blues and oranges, contrast the crows' calm self-containment with Coyote's outrageous lack of control. See, too, Paul Goble's many stories about the Plains Native American trickster Iktomi, which entice audiences to participate in the humorous stories much as the original listeners did when the stories were told.

## Dogzilla

BY DAV PILKEY
HARCOURT, 1993. (I)

Dogzilla, a huge but benign-looking mutt, invades Mousopolis in this take-off on horror movies. Humor is in the silly situation as much as in the collage illustrations that combine photographs and painted backgrounds. The author presents another canine hero with a problem in *Dog Breath!: The Horrible Trouble with Hally Tosis* (Scholastic, 1994). Not even cats are safe from Pilkey's wild imagination in the feline parody of horror films, *Kat Kong* (Harcourt, 1993). Reluctant readers, and boys particularly, laugh at the silly humor in Pilkey's comic book-like series starring Captain Underpants (published by Scholastic).

## Double Fudge

BY JUDY BLUME
DUTTON, 2002. (I, U)

Peter, his little brother Fudge, and their parents are back! When Fudge becomes obsessed with money, the family visits the Bureau of Engraving in Washington, D.C. There, they run into long lost relatives who return with them for an extended stay back in New York. Snappy dialogue, recognizable situations, and (mostly!) likeable characters make this a worthy companion to *Superfudge* (1980) and *Fudge-a-Mania* (1990, both Dutton). (Series)

## Fair Weather

BY RICHARD PECK
DIAL, 2001. (U)

The Becketts rarely venture off their Illinois farm, until Aunt Euterpe's letter arrives inviting the family to the 1893 World's Fair. Rosie, her siblings, and their eccentric grandfather travel by train to Chicago, which, according to Rosie, is filled mostly with criminals. Readers see the Fair through Rosie's narration and find out more about the real granddad. Plot twists and quirky characters, some based on real people, are humorous and engaging.

## Farmer Duck

BY MARTIN WADDELL
ILLUSTRATED BY HELEN OXENBURY
CANDLEWICK, 1991. (P)

While doing all of the work for a lazy farmer, Duck nearly collapses from his difficult labors. So the animals get together, chase the farmer away, and run the farm themselves. Children will chant, "How goes the work?" and answer "Quack" along with the reader. The book compares well with versions of the "Little Red Hen" to use in talking about work and the consequences of not helping.

## Four Famished Foxes and Fosdyke

BY PAMELA DUNCAN EDWARDS
ILLUSTRATED BY HENRY COLE
HARPERCOLLINS, 1995. (P, I)

Fosdyke the chief fox is left in charge of his siblings who escape to forage in the farmyard. Cole has cleverly tucked many objects starting with the letter 'F' into the pictures to perfectly match a story that relies heavily on words beginning with that letter. Other alliterative romps include *Dinorella* (Hyperion, 1997), *Some Smug Slug* (1996) and *Clara Caterpillar* (2001, both HarperCollins).

## Fox on Wheels

BY EDWARD MARSHALL
ILLUSTRATED BY JAMES MARSHALL
DIAL, 1983. (P, I)

Fox is a memorable character who is forever getting in and out of trouble. Here he babysits his sister, climbs a tree for grapes, and has a race with a shopping cart. Newly independent readers will appreciate the humor in the understated text and engaging depictions of Fox and friends in comic line-and-wash illustrations. The same team also created *Three by the Sea* (Dial, 1981), a riotous tale of friends telling stories to each other while at the beach. (Series)

## The Frog Wore Red Suspenders

BY JACK PRELUTSKY
ILLUSTRATED BY PETRA MATHERS
GREENWILLOW, 2002. (P, I)

Prelutsky's rhymes fairly trip off the reader's tongue and invite children to chime in, memorize, and quote the funny parts to each other. As in many of his poetry collections, geography figures heavily—a hen stuck at the bottom of the Grand Canyon, Peanut Peg and Peanut Pete, who meet on a sunny Atlanta street, and Winnie Appleton, who bounces her ball from Minneapolis to St. Paul. This book offers a great introduction to the poet most children like best after Shel Silverstein and is a fitting choice to pair with and lighten up intermediate U.S. geography studies.

## The Great Chicken Debacle

BY PHYLLIS REYNOLDS NAYLOR
MARSHALL CAVENDISH, 2001. (I, U)

At their father's request, the Morgan children secretly care for a chicken throughout the week before their mother's birthday. If they're successful, the bird will be a surprise gift and the kids will get a trip to an amusement park. The deal is threatened when a not-too-nefarious gang kidnaps the chicken. A peculiar premise is delightfully executed in this silly novel.

## The Great White Man-Eating Shark

BY MARGARET MAHY
ILLUSTRATED BY JONATHAN ALLEN
DIAL, 1991. (P, I)

A selfish boy, Norvin, looks very much like a shark, and when he has to share Carmel Cove with other swimmers, he becomes resentful and cross. So he disguises himself with fins and scares all the other swimmers out of the water. This works until a lovely female shark spots Norvin. With absolutely deadpan humor, the author tells what happens when a plain boy shapes up into a rather good-looking shark.

## How Tom Beat Captain Najork and His Hired Sportsmen

BY RUSSELL HOBAN
ILLUSTRATED BY QUENTIN BLAKE
ATHENEUM, 1974. (I)

A celebration of "messing around" and its ultimate rewards, this classic book is temporarily out of print. But it's worth tracking down for its earnest and hilarious account of how Tom's guardian, Aunt Fidget Wonkham-Strong, hires a team of four British sportsmen headed by the notorious Captain Najork to defeat Tom and force him to be serious. But with his abilities to fool around, Tom brilliantly plays "womble, muck, and sneedball," beats them all, marries his battle-ax aunt to Captain Najork, and finds a new guardian. The book has also a not-so-sneaky message about "wasting" time.

## Little Wolf's Book of Badness

BY IAN WHYBROW
ILLUSTRATED BY TONY ROSS
CAROLRHODA, 1999. (I)

In letters to his parents, Little Wolf describes the school where he has landed, the Cunning College for Brute Beasts run by his Uncle Bigbad. With hopes of earning his BAD badge, Little Wolf reports each adventure in naive, ink-splatted letters with Tom-Swift-like closings that make readers laugh with recognition because they know what Little Wolf will discover—that Uncle Bigbad is not a good guy. Whybrow's next book reveals how Little Wolf eventually gains control of the school. (Series)

## Martha Speaks

BY SUSAN MEDDAUGH
HOUGHTON MIFFLIN, 1992. (P)

Martha is a dog who, when fed alphabet soup, experiences something astonishing. Instead of the letters going to her stomach, they go to her brain and, voilà!, Martha can speak! Humorous line-and-wash sketches depict a lumpy Martha who is at first amazed, then thrilled with her new ability. Readers will learn what she thinks and says in dialogue balloons that accompany the cartoon-like illustrations. (Series)

## McBroom's Wonderful One-Acre Farm: Three Tall Tales

BY SID FLEISCHMAN
ILLUSTRATED BY QUENTIN BLAKE
BEECH TREE BOOKS, 1997. (I)

Here, the author retells three tall tales about modern folk hero Josh McBroom and his amazing farm. On McBroom's farm, the soil is so rich that plants spring from the ground and trees sprout nickels that grow into quarters. But this exuberant growing isn't without problems for the resourceful farmer. Filled with puns and exaggeration, as are traditional tall tales, these stories about McBroom are as funny to contemporary readers as they were to their original audience in the 1960s. Discussing the hilarious Mr. McBroom will remind young readers of other tall tales they have read in which humor enters the story riding on the coattails of exaggeration. (Series)

## Minerva Louise at School

BY JANET STOEKE
DUTTON, 1996. (P)

Minerva Louise, a chicken, mistakes all of the kindergarten classroom details for her common farmyard accoutrements. A wastebasket is understood to be a feeding trough, cubbies are nesting boxes, and a baseball glove and ball become a nest with eggs. It's all very funny for young children who have insider knowledge. This is a good precursor to Peggy Parrish's *Amelia Bedelia* books for slightly older readers. (Series)

## Minnie and Moo Save the Earth

BY DENYS CAZET
DORLING KINDERSLEY, 1999. (P, I)

While enjoying a picnic and a soak in the farmer's hot tub, two bovine friends are annoyed by mosquitoes, really aliens who mistake the cows for the earth's dominant inhabitants. Cazet's easy-reader stories combine silly, improbable situations with funny details and a witty telling whose allusions, references, and puns might be lost on very young readers but can be appreciated by most second graders. (Series)

## Once Upon a Marigold

BY JERRY FERRIS
HARCOURT, 2002. (U)

Stock characters from fairy tales assume lead roles (and become individuals) in this richly textured novel, which includes "everything but the kitchen sink." Spunky Christian runs away at a young age, is taken in by a troll named Edric, and falls in love with Princess Marigold, who is in danger from her evil stepmother, Queen Olympia. The complex plot plays with words, ideas, allusions, and even mixes up genres for a very funny and very satisfying outcome.

## Skinnybones

BY BARBARA PARK
RANDOM HOUSE, 1997. (I, U)

Updated from the 1982 edition, this easy-to-read novel tells of wisecracking Alex, the smallest player on the baseball team, and his annual trials with the team bully. A subplot involves Alex's attempts to win a cat food commercial contest, beginning in the first chapter with his wildly inventive story to his mother about how kibbles spilled on the kitchen floor. This chapter makes a great read-aloud and will propel even reluctant readers into the book. Alex's story continues in *Almost Starring Skinnybones* (Random House, 1995).

## The Stories Julian Tells

BY ANN CAMERON
ILLUSTRATED BY ANN STUGNELL
PANTHEON, 1981. (I)

There's gentle humor in everyday activities as readers learn when they meet Julian and his younger brother, Huey. Here, Julian looses a tooth, plants a garden, tries to grow taller, and sometimes exaggerates. The author got the idea for this volume from a real-life Julian who, told of his childhood in South Africa and a time when he and his brother decided to take just a little taste of a grand pudding their father had made for their mother. One nibble led to another until nothing was left, except the story that inspired this book. Each evocative chapter can be read individually or as part of a whole story. (Series)

## Summer Reading Is Killing Me

BY JON SCIESZKA
ILLUSTRATED BY LANE SMITH
VIKING, 1998. (I)

The "Time Warp Trio" find themselves inside a Daniel Pinkwater book, *The Hoboken Chicken Emergency* (1977; Aladdin, 1999), and under siege from evil characters in other children's books. Can they find "The Book," the magical portal that will allow them to return to the present? Readers will recognize many book allusions and might survey each other to see which titles are most popular. A "summer reading list" and a silly study guide seem just right for third and fourth graders. (Series)

## Take Me Out of the Bathtub and Other Silly Dilly Songs

BY ALAN KATZ
ILLUSTRATED BY DAVID CATROW
McELDERRY, 2001. (I, U)

Outlandish illustrations accompany fourteen parodies of well-known songs. "I've Been Cleaning Up My Bedroom," sung to the tune of "I've Been Working on the Railroad," shows how a girl accomplishes this task by emptying her belongings onto the lawn. It's the exaggerated, over-the-top feeling of these poems that makes readers laugh. The rewritten songs are fun to sing and, for some groups, a jump start to writing similar parodies of other songs.

### The True Story of the Three Little Pigs by A. Wolf

AS TOLD TO JON SCIESZKA
ILLUSTRATED BY LANE SMITH
VIKING, 1989. (I)

Is it his fault he's been so deeply maligned? He only wanted to borrow a cup of sugar for his poor old granny. This now-classic take on the "Three Little Pigs," as told from the "victimized" wolf's point of view, relies on a child's knowledge of the story on which it's based. Taking a new perspective on an old story shows up in many skewed versions of folktales. Collecting these twisted variants and noticing how the author or illustrator has tinkered with the original not only resurrects old tales for one more telling but also encourages readers to talk about how stories relate to each other.

### Tough Cookie

BY DAVID WISNIEWSKI
LOTHROP, LEE, & SHEPARD, 1999. (I)

This cookie is a trench-coat wearing private investigator, a P.I. who came from a good "top of the jar" family. He's got a girl named Pecan Sandy and a buddy named Chips. Collage illustrations perfectly match the clipped sentences filled with puns and language play that spoof detective stories and delight readers. Wisniewski again demonstrates his offbeat humor when he reveals *The Secret Knowledge of Grownups* (Lothrop, 1998) (I).

### Wait! No Paint

BY BRUCE WHATLEY
HARPERCOLLINS, 2001. (P, I)

This comical farce starts as a traditional retelling of the familiar "Three Little Pigs," but it soon becomes a stage for interaction between a realistically portrayed illustrator intruding into the book and the cartoonish pigs he draws. The artist's tools are shown on the page as the pigs complain about the artist's techniques and the color he's using. Pair this with David Weisner's *The Three Pigs* (Chapter 10) in which various characters also escape the limiting boundaries of their stories.

### The Web Files

BY MARGIE PALATINI
ILLUSTRATED BY RICHARD EGIELSKI
HYPERION, 2001. (I)

In a mystery parody full of puns and allusions to both nursery rhymes and terse detective bits from television shows like "Dragnet," Ductective Webb and his sidekick solve the mystery of who's stealing vegetables. Older children will appreciate the many media and literary references, and some may even imitate this genre by rewriting a folktale as a detective story.

### Wolf!

BY BECKY BLOOM
ILLUSTRATED BY PASCAL BIET
ORCHARD, 1999. (P)

When a hungry wolf lunges at some animals in the farmyard, they ignore him because he's interrupted their reading. Annoyed, the wolf decides to look into this "reading" and after a few hilarious false starts, he finally gets it. In the bargain, he discovers his storytelling prowess, a new occupation, and makes some new, no longer edible, friends. There's wisdom in this spoof, and it gets children to talk about strategies for good reading. Readers might list other good wolf or bad wolf stories as a way of looking back on patterns in their own reading accomplishments.

### The Wonderful O

BY JAMES THURBER
SIMON & SCHUSTER, 1957. (U)

A pirate named Black lands on the island of Ooroo and decides to banish the letter "O"—in both upper and lower case, of course. The play on language is a hoot (a word that couldn't exist on the island until the islanders take a stand). Thurber provides a gentle lesson about the power of other words with this vowel—such as love, hope and valor—that will have readers thinking about other essential words, whether grouped by "O" or any other vowel or consonant.

# Chapter 8

# Getting THROUGH Tough Times

Author Katherine Paterson tells the story of coming upon a terrible fire with her young son. As they watched the fire rage, fear engulfed her child. Seeking to comfort him, Paterson encouraged her son to "Look for the helpers." This reassuring phrase reminded him, as it reminds us, that in the toughest times, there are always helpers—brave, courageous people who, through small acts and generous gestures, help us persevere.

Whether facing a great tragedy or confronting a simple dread, everyone experiences difficult times. For children, it may be surviving the first sleepover at a friend's house or dealing with nightmares. It might be the terror of thunder and lightning or losing a loved one or pet. Scary headlines jump out from the daily newspaper and blare from the television. Across the globe, children experience poverty and hunger, violence and illiteracy, riots and wars. As much as we wish to protect children from life's harsh realities, the hard times still come around, again and again.

Why, then, should we read books about difficult times? Why borrow another's trouble? Shouldn't we read happy books that preserve the simple joys of childhood as long as possible?

While it would be wonderful if we could protect all children from tough times, we can't. We can only give them the tools of compassion and hope and the possibility of responsible actions.

Like first responders on the scene, books can be helpers. Many of the books in this chapter deal with common childhood fears. Ed Emberley's *Go Away, Big Green Monster* shows how the reader creates, and then defeats, scary thoughts. Other books, such as Kate Lied's *Potato: A Tale from the Great Depression*, use a historical backdrop to spotlight the courage of people who faced daunting circumstances. And there are reflective works that invite discussion and thought, such as *This Place I Know: Poems of Comfort* by Georgia Heard, poems collected in the aftermath of the September 11, 2001, attacks.

## Fighting Fear

On September 11, 2001, my son was just seven years old. The images, horror, and grief were hard enough for me to handle. For a seven-year-old, the tragedy and its aftermath were overwhelming. My son asked me lots of questions about what had happened, then he did something surprising. He searched the house until he found three picture books that had been his favorites in kindergarten and preschool, and he read and reread them—alone and with me. I realized that these books put him in control; that in each of them, a fierce monster was subdued or outwitted by a seemingly weaker character. Though my son couldn't control the outside world, books helped give him the courage and confidence to control that scariest of monsters—his own fear.

**JIM BRENNAN**
**PARENT OF A 9-YEAR-OLD**

Within these books are tales in which music, an object or talisman reminiscent of a loved one, a generous policeman, a story-telling grandmother, worthwhile work and the passing of time are helpers to characters faced with hard times. Reading about people who have overcome small difficulties or survived unimaginable ones can help children develop compassion and empathy for those who have struggled. Equally as important, these books suggest possibilities that help children learn to look forward, move beyond, get through.

The books in this chapter share one strong thread—the belief that things will get better. In each case, a child comes through a disappointing, scary, difficult experience and is stronger for the journey. Sometimes an adult or an older friend provides help and guidance. But always, the child finds the strength within to persevere and grow, in ways big and small.

Look for the helpers.

**EVE BUNTING** *is the author of more than 150 books for children and young adults, including **Smoky Night** and **The Wall**. Known for her sensitive treatments of even the most complex and wrenching topics, Bunting has created books that show children and young adults they're not alone in the troubles they face. Bunting's books, like a dear friend, offer comfort, counsel, and a dose of reality.*

**You're not afraid to tackle tough topics. Why is it important for you to write about these issues?**

It's important because I know that kids can and do face up to issues such as poverty, discrimination, illiteracy, and homelessness. For some children, this is all they know and I don't want them to feel alone. It isn't always easy, writing about injustice or poverty, but it is oh, so necessary.

# RECOMMENDED Books

P = PRIMARY (KINDERGARTEN – GRADE 3)
I = INTERMEDIATE (GRADE 3 – GRADE 4)
U = UPPER (GRADE 4 – GRADE 6)

## Amber Was Brave, Essie Was Smart

BY VERA B. WILLIAMS
GREENWILLOW, 2001. (I, U)

Amber and Essie are sisters, each with her own particular strength as together they deal with tough times. It's gradually revealed through poetry in free verse that the girls' father is in jail for check forgery, their mother works long hours, and the radiators are often cold. Sketches in color and black and white portray the family—and depict a hopeful ending as the children open their door and find their father on the other side. The unique strengths of each family member and how they factor into this moving family album is likely to create gentle laughter as well as quiet sniffles.

## Blackberries in the Dark

BY MAVIS JUKES
ILLUSTRATED BY THOMAS B. ALLEN
KNOPF, 2001 (1985). (I)

Austin is spending the summer with Grandma, but life hasn't been the same since Grandpa died. Yet, as Austin and Gram visit old places, gather courage to try out Grandpa's favorite hobby of fly fishing, and handle family treasures, they rekindle old traditions and start some new ones in this comforting story of grief, love, and beginning again. This is a good book for talking about family treasures and what they mean to us.

## Blues Journey

BY WALTER DEAN MYERS
ILLUSTRATED BY CHRISTOPHER MYERS
HOLIDAY HOUSE, 2003. (U)

Poems inspired by blues music and musicians are illustrated in shades of blue. Together, language and art convey the tone, emotion, and some actual history of the African-American experience. This powerful work by father and son will lead to questions and discussion about the history of the United States and about the role of music in its documentation. The story also begs readers to listen to the blues with paper and a box of blue-hued crayons in front of them.

## The Breadwinner

BY DEBORAH ELLIS
GROUNDWOOD BOOKS, 2001. (U)

Parvana is the 11-year-old daughter of university-educated parents living in Afghanistan under Taliban rule. When her father is taken away because of his education, Parvana dresses as a boy and becomes the family breadwinner. Readers will empathize with Parvana, glimpse a difficult daily life in a contemporary time period, and perhaps begin to understand more about Afghanistan. *Camel Bells* by Janne Carlsson, translated by Angela Barnett-Lindberg (Groundwood Books, 2002) takes a look at life in Afghanistan before the Taliban through the eyes of Hajdar, a twelve-year-old boy.

## The Broken Cat

BY LYNNE RAE PERKINS
HARPERCOLLINS, 2002. (P, I)

Two stories interweave to illustrate how narratives comfort us when we're ill or worried. Andy's cat, Frank, is wounded and, while Andy apprehensively waits for the vet to appear, he asks his mother, grandmother, and aunt to tell the story about when his mother broke her arm years ago. In the story retold in the vet's waiting room, Andy's mom's arm finally healed. And sure enough, Frank recovers from his head injury as well. Ask readers to talk and write about anxious times with their own family pets or a time when stories provided comfort.

## Courage

BY BERNARD WABER
HOUGHTON MIFFLIN, 2002. (P, I)

This cartoon-style catalogue of all the ways people show courage ranges through physical acts, like jumping off the high board at the pool or riding without training wheels, to challenging situations, like introducing yourself to a group of strangers or keeping "face" when you arrive too early at a party. Waber's comic depiction of emotions, and the silly as well as serious examples of courageous acts, are sure to start conversations about the differences between mental and physical courage and the grandstand play versus quiet heroism. The theme and humorous format of this picture book make it useful in generating conversation with older readers, too.

## Dakota Dugout

BY ANN TURNER
ILLUSTRATED BY RON HIMLER
SIMON & SCHUSTER, 1985. (P, I)

A woman, now settled in a town, recalls her life as a bride living in a sod house on the plains. Black and white illustrations help communicate the isolation on the vast open prairie and can lead to talk about different kinds of isolation, the role of friendship and family in mitigating loneliness, and how loneliness and isolation can occur in any setting in any time period.

## Flamingo Dream

BY DONNA JO NAPOLI
ILLUSTRATED BY CATHIE FELSTEAD
GREENWILLOW, 2002. (P, I)

The narrator collects things to put in an album as she recalls her trip to Florida with her father before he died of cancer. She and her mother realize that she's made her own "Year Book" and is now ready to put words to her sorrow and grief in losing her father and also to her joyous memories of him. Brightly colored illustrations incorporate child-like art into textured, layered collage pictures that will generate discussion of keepsakes and how one remembers a person who is lost to them. Loss of a parent is also explored in *Kisses from Rosa* by Petra Mathers (Knopf, 1995), a story in which a girl is separated from and finally reunited with a mother recuperating from tuberculosis. In their letters to each other, they send butterfly kisses along with love and hope.

## Gershon's Monster

BY ERIC KIMMEL
ILLUSTRATED BY JON J. MUTH
SCHOLASTIC, 2000. (I)

Selfish Gershon commits plenty of little sins (shown as small black shapes) that he sweeps into the basement of his bakery and later disposes of in the sea. His refusal to own up to these transgressions causes a huge monster to rear up from the ocean. And then Gershon must truly repent. This Hasidic legend of atonement invites children to talk about occasions for making up, saying "I'm sorry," and other conciliatory gestures that keep families, classrooms, or friendships in balance.

## Go Away, Big Green Monster

BY ED EMBERLEY
LITTLE, BROWN, 1993. (P)

In die-cut pages, readers construct a monster from imagination and then deconstruct it as they turn the pages. It's a very simple and supportive book for helping young children talk about how we can control our imaginations and stay in charge, even if scary thoughts sometimes overtake us. This book is a crafts project waiting to happen. Encourage children to construct their own monsters with markers and paper or cardboard or collage and then make a positive change by adding a flip-back cheerful head and other changeable features. Ask children to talk about how they can control their monster by taking its shape apart, just like in the book.

## Grandmother Bryant's Pocket

BY JACQUELINE BRIGGS MARTIN
ILLUSTRATED BY PETRA MATHERS
HOUGHTON MIFFLIN, 1996. (I)

In this beautiful, small book set in 1787, Sarah suffers from nightmares after her dog Patches is killed in a barn fire. So she goes to stay with her grandmother. Time and work combine to help her overcome her grief, and her actions in helping a mean-spirited neighbor earn Sarah a new cat for a pet. The grandmother's gifts of a pocket embroidered with "Fear Not," and comforting talisman herbs to tuck inside, also help. This is a good story for talking about going forward with work and friends as time works its magic. Readers may share stories about things that have scared them and the talismans or special stuffed animals that provided comfort.

## Hatchet

BY GARY PAULSEN
MACMILLAN, 1986. (U)

This rugged story of Brian, whose plane crashes in the Canadian wilderness, killing the pilot and leaving the boy stranded, has become a modern classic. Brian evolves from a spoiled and angry boy to a truly self-sufficient one through a series of mistakes, planning, and luck before he is rescued. In the process, readers can consider the qualities a person needs to survive; the role of art, beauty, and memory in surviving; and what a person learns from survival. These threads are found in numerous survival stories across genres, and older readers will enjoy comparing characters and the way they deal with the challenges they face. (Series)

## Iris and Walter: The School Play

BY ELISSA HADEN GUEST
ILLUSTRATED BY CHRISTINE DAVENIER
HARCOURT, 2003 (P)

Best friends Iris and Walter are going to be bugs in the school play and excitedly tell everyone in the family who'll listen. Iris practices her lines and even reassuringly helps Walter when he forgets his at the dress rehearsal. But disaster strikes when Iris is sick with a fever on the day of the play and misses the excitement of the performance. It's difficult to return to school and hear all about the successful venture, but Walter and an empathetic teacher help her through the day. This comforting story suggests that there's always another chance and that friends come through for each other. Iris loses her courage but lives through another childhood hard time sweetly recounted in *Iris and Walter: The Sleepover* (Harcourt, 2002).

## Just Juice

BY KAREN HESSE
ILLUSTRATED BY ROBERT ANDREW PARKER
SCHOLASTIC, 1998. (U)

Nine-year-old Juice tells the story of how illiteracy and poverty have affected her rural family. Her father, who can't read, is out of work, back taxes on their house are long overdue, her diabetic mother is pregnant, and it looks like the family will go under. But Juice's spirited rallying of her father, her help in delivering her new sister, the family's acceptance of some assistance from a social worker, and learning to read all play a part in restoring hope. Among the many ideas in this warm book are the role of education in moving out of poverty and the way hard times call up acts of courage.

## The Little Old Lady Who Wasn't Afraid of Anything

BY LINDA WILLIAMS
ILLUSTRATED BY MEGAN LLOYD
HARPERCOLLINS, 1986. (P)

Perfect for chanting and ideal for newly proficient readers, this picture book features a lady who outfaces scary shoes going "CLOMP, CLOMP," a pumpkin head that shouts "BOO," and some menacing clothes. In the end, the lady creates a scarecrow to frighten away crows. Children might dramatize this cumulative narrative with props and give voice to a story that demonstrates quietly that boldness counts.

## Once Upon a Time

BY NIKI DALY

FARRAR, STRAUS & GIROUX, 2003. (P)

Sarie dreads having to read aloud in her South African school because the words just seem to dance in front of her eyes. But when she visits her Auntie Annie who lives across the veldt, they snuggle in a no-wheeled, dilapidated car to read the old *Cinderella* book Sarie has found wedged between the seats. With the help of her wise aunt and a new friend at school, Sarie builds up her confidence and becomes a successful reader. Daly's watercolors of the Karoo region of South Africa create a beautiful picture of this area. The book pairs well with Katherine Paterson's story about another child who overcomes reading difficulties with help from a family member, *Marvin One Too Many*, in Chapter 2.

## Pictures of Hollis Woods

BY PATRICIA REILLY GIFF

WENDY LAMB BOOKS/RANDOM HOUSE, 2002. (U)

Hollis Woods, abandoned at birth and so named for the place she was born, keeps running away from foster homes. When placed with Josie, an older woman who's an artist, Hollis feels an almost immediate connection, though it's clear that Josie is slipping into dementia. Pictures Hollis recalls and others she creates reveal how she once perceived family and what she now believes it to be. This hopeful, moving novel is constructed in such a way that flashbacks become understandable to less experienced readers. A lighter hopeful story about foster children is *Ruby Holler* by Sharon Creech, in Chapter 6.

## Poppy

BY AVI

ILLUSTRATED BY BRIAN FLOCA

ORCHARD BOOKS, 1995. (I)

Poppy the mouse exhibits all kinds of bravery in thought and action as she confronts Mr. Ocax the owl, who grants mice the privilege of using a field. Readers will enjoy cataloging the increasingly brave steps Poppy takes in developing courage and can discuss how bravery isn't always in actions. Avi's colorful language is worth noting, as are his use of foreshadowing, descriptive passages, and the hilarious porcupine curses. (Series)

## Potato: A Tale from the Great Depression

BY KATE LIED

ILLUSTRATED BY LISA CAMPBELL ERNST

NATIONAL GEOGRAPHIC, 1997. (P, I)

The author was eight years old when she wrote this story about her grandparents' early married life. To make it through the Depression in the 1930s, they moved from Kansas to Idaho with their baby daughter to find work picking potatoes and then returned home with a carload of produce to barter. The simple story illustrates the writing principle of telling well one small incident when you write a family story. The tale should also inspire readers to write their own stories of getting through tough times.

## Skeleton Man

BY JOSEPH BRUCHAC

HARPERCOLLINS, 2001. (U)

Molly must rely on her strength and wit as she deals with missing parents, a mysterious and rather threatening uncle, and confusing dreams about the Skeleton Man, a character in a traditional Mohawk story she heard from her father. This taut and scary novel is told in Molly's voice in the present tense so the reader learns what happens at the same time Molly does. Children will find it interesting to exchange opinions about the book's style and tone, the heroine's actions, and the Mohawk traditions woven throughout the story.

## Smoky Night

BY EVE BUNTING

ILLUSTRATED BY DAVID DIAZ

HARCOURT BRACE, 1994. (P, I)

When the Los Angeles riots break out in the streets of their neighborhood, a boy and his mother leave their burning apartment house and find safety and courage in the community. The potentially frightening subject is overshadowed by reassuring helpers: the boy's protective mother, the policeman, and a cat-owning neighbor formerly not trusted by the small family. Note Diaz's choice of collage material and how it supports the content of the story.

## Sometimes Bad Things Happen

BY ELLEN JACKSON
PHOTOGRAPHS BY SHELLEY ROTNER
MILLBROOK PRESS, 2002. (P)

In expressive photographs and simple text, this book calls attention to how we feel and behave when bad and scary things happen—anything from losing a game to losing someone you love. The author takes a subtle approach and resulting conversation may ultimately end, as the book does, with the reassurance that the world is full of good and helpful people who can comfort in times of trouble.

## The Steps

BY RACHEL COHN
SIMON & SCHUSTER, 2003. (U)

Annabel's father not only married a woman with other children, but also started a new family halfway across the world in Australia. Annabel's often-humorous narration tells her story of traveling to Australia, her jealousy of the new family, and her fear that she's lost her place in her father's heart. Gradually, she realizes that she has her own special place in this large family. Readers might discuss how blended families change, grow, and move geographically, as well as how feelings of jealousy and impermanence can evolve into something more positive.

## This Place I Know: Poems of Comfort

SELECTED BY GEORGIA HEARD
ILLUSTRATED BY EIGHTEEN RENOWNED PICTURE BOOK ARTISTS
CANDLEWICK PRESS, 2002. (P, I, U)

The editor begins by noting, "During difficult times, we all need a place where the heart can rest." This collection of poems, gathered in response to the World Trade Center tragedy, provides a beautiful starting point for a supportive discussion in any time of sadness, confusion, fear, or loss. These poems help readers consider what words and actions provide comfort. Artists such as Peter Sís, Petra Mathers, Giselle Potter, and Shane Evans contribute visual metaphors in a variety of media that enhance and deepen the poems' meanings.

## Thunder Cake

BY PATRICIA POLACCO
PHILOMEL, 1990. (P)

As a child, the author was deeply afraid of thunder. Here, she tells a story of how her babushka, her Ukrainian grandmother, helped her get over her fear by making a Thunder Cake. As an impending storm moves closer to their farm, the two of them scurry to collect eggs and milk, which, her grandmother points out, is a very brave thing to do. After all the measuring and stirring, by the time the cake is ready and the storm hits, the child has forgotten to be afraid. Readers can talk about overcoming fear by staying busy and they just might want to bake a cake with a recipe the author has included. The humorous story *Storm Is Coming*, by Heather Tekavec, illustrated by Margaret Spengler (Dial, 2002), shows how naive farm animals mistakenly interpret the overheard "storm is coming" as a warning of a fearsome person's arrival.

## Tornado

BY BETSY BYARS
ILLUSTRATED BY DORON BEN-AMI
HARPERCOLLINS, 1996. (I)

With a tornado bearing down, the family and their hired man Pete crowd into their prairie root cellar. But they worry about the narrator's daddy who is trapped outside. Pete tells stories about his dog Tornado, comfortable familiar ones the children have heard before, as the storm beats down, and when it ends, there is daddy. In this very short novel, Pete's stories are humorous and even sad but always riveting. Family stories are often told at difficult times; readers might like to talk about the comfort stories provide in their lives. Factual information can be equally reassuring, such as that found in the informational books of Seymour Simon. *Tornadoes* (Morrow, 1999), *Lightning* (Morrow, 1997), and other titles in Simon's weather series, use topnotch photographs and lucid text to demystify naturally occurring events.

## Visiting Day

BY JACQUELINE WOODSON
ILLUSTRATED BY JAMES E. RANSOME
SCHOLASTIC, 2002. (P, I)

The narrator and her grandmother prepare for a bus trip to see the girl's father who is "doing a little time." Dad, a handsome man in khaki, also eagerly anticipates his daughter's visit. Only illustrations denote that he is actually incarcerated. These richly colored pictures and the straightforward text focus on the joyful meeting and hopeful eventual reunion, not the cause of the separation, and encourage discussion of the difficulty of being apart from a loved one.

## When Vera Was Sick

BY VERA ROSENBERRY
HENRY HOLT, 1996. (P)

Vera catches the measles, has to stay in a darkened room with scary wallpaper, and can't sleep. But gradually, with the help of her mother who reads to her and other family members who offer support, she gets better. Recovering from illness takes a certain amount of hope and reassurance that often comes from routines, people, or unique distractions. Ask children how they keep up their spirits during an illness or help cheer others who are sick. (Series)

## Willow and Twig

BY JEAN LITTLE
VIKING, 2003. (FIRST PUBLISHED IN CANADA, 2000) (U)

Willow and her younger brother, Twig, are on their own again when their drug-addicted mother takes off. After a social worker contacts their grandmother in Ontario, Willow begins to remember her early life when she and her mother lived with Willow's grandmother on the other side of Canada. When the children join their grandmother, she gradually helps Willow realize she's no longer alone in keeping the family together and dealing with Twig's learning disabilities. The foibles and strengths of each memorable character should generate discussion as will the obstacles each must overcome to grow, to become a real family, to make friends, and to accept people with their peculiarities and problems.

## Interactive Books

As a school counselor, I'm always looking for ways to help children deal with feelings of anxiety, grief, or anger. I may have to help students who've been fighting in class, whose parents are getting a divorce, or who've just lost a grandparent. I have an interactive book that's especially helpful for students who are dealing with grief. At the top of each page is a question. In the middle of the page is a picture the child can color. A sentence at the bottom of the page explains what happening in the picture. And at the back of the book is a place for a child to write his or her own story. We go through each page together, and by the time we finish the book, my student usually feels calmer. This book has been such a useful tool that I'm planning on creating one myself tailored to some of the other challenges my students face.

GAIL LIGGINS
GUIDANCE COUNSELOR
ADAMS ELEMENTARY SCHOOL
WASHINGTON, D.C.

# Chapter 9

# Making A Difference

When did you first realize you could change the world or at least your corner of the world? How did you learn you could make a difference? As adults, we leave our fingerprints on the world in countless ways each day. We vote. We build. We rear children. We teach. We're policy makers, civic leaders, and community volunteers, accustomed to the idea that the world changes because of the decisions we make.

But children, just discovering the world around them, are not at all sure they can rearrange much of anything. They're used to the idea that grownups make all the decisions. Even when confronted with a situation they know needs changing, a young person might feel, just as Alice does in Barbara Cooney's *Miss Rumphius*, "What can I do? How can I make a difference?"

Books can lead the way by depicting examples and role models that challenge and inspire. These stories show that even the youngest child has the power to make small steps that can lead to great change. Strong characters and compelling stories help young readers discover the many ways people identify problems, make tough decisions, resolve conflicts, find solutions, or right a wrong.

The books in this section were selected with these qualities in mind. They show children the power they have to make a difference—from prompting a simple change of heart to altering world events. In Sharon Wyeth's *Something Beautiful*, a young girl is determined to make the world a better place, starting with her own backyard. In Ken Mochizuki's *Passage to Freedom: The Sugihara Story*, a son watches his father courageously defy his government and save the lives of thousands. In the autobiographical sketch,

*I Am Rosa Parks*, a brave African-American woman strikes a blow against racial discrimination with a defiant gesture that sparks the modern Civil Rights movement. In Russell Freedman's *Out of Darkness: The Story of Louis Braille*, a 15-year-old blind boy invents a system of lettering that becomes the universal written language for people who are visually impaired. These individuals shaped the world, for themselves and others, by following their dreams and holding to their beliefs.

## Turning On A Light

It's amazing what impact printed words on a page can have on someone's life. An author combines just the right words and turns on a light inside the reader. I taught a troubled student who had been kicked out of every school he attended. Justin, whose mother was addicted to crack, worked double duty as the leader of a gang and the caretaker of his five-year-old brother. After I read *More Than Anything Else*, Marie Bradby's book about the young Booker T. Washington, aloud in class, I noticed Justin began to change. I asked my students to write a paper about what they wanted more than anything else and saw the light turn on in Justin. He wrote that he wanted to be "somebody." So, he began his journey—he left the gang, became a straight-A student, and used his abilities to become a leader in our school and community. I know that one book can't change a person's life, but the right book at the right time made an incredible difference to Justin.

**TAMMY DORSTEN**
**READING TEACHER**
**KENNESAW ELEMENTARY SCHOOL**
**KENNESAW, GEORGIA**

There's a bumper sticker that reads "Life Is Not a Spectator Sport." As children talk about the books in this chapter, with each other and with the adults they know, the words on that bumper sticker will start to make a lot of sense. In all of these stories, young people and adults become catalysts for change—in their schools, jobs, neighborhoods, communities, towns, and cities. Children will see that, like the people in the stories, they, too, can leave their unique fingerprints on the world in which they live.

Photo: Michelle Litvir

*Heroism is a common thread among many of author* **KEN MOCHIZUKI'S** *books, from the small heroes of* **Baseball Saved Us** *to the Japanese ambassador who saved thousands of lives with the simple strokes of his pen in* **Passage to Freedom**. *Here, Mochizuki talks about the difference one simple act can make.*

**Your books continue to inspire readers with their stories of simple acts of courage. How has writing them inspired you?**

Chiune Sugihara has become one of my personal heroes because of his willingness to risk his life and career to save others. The more I learned, the more I became inspired by this courageous man. But you don't have to be an ambassador to change people's lives. I wanted these books to show that one person, one act of bravery, one sacrifice or effort to stand strong can indeed make a difference.

# RECOMMENDED B⌀⌀KS

P = Primary (Kindergarten – Grade 3)
I = Intermediate (Grade 3 – Grade 4)
U = Upper (Grade 4 – Grade 6)

## A Band of Angels: A Story Inspired by the Jubilee Singers

BY DEBORAH HOPKINSON
ILLUSTRATED BY RAÚL COLÓN
ATHENEUM, 1999. (I, U)

Based on true events, this is the story of Ella, who used a gift of great beauty—her singing voice—to save her debt-ridden school. Born in 1851 into slavery in Nashville, Tennessee, Ella is freed when her father is able to buy his family's freedom. Ella works as a laundress and saves enough money to go to Fisk College, a school established in 1866 to offer a college education to newly freed slaves. But Fisk is teetering on the brink financially. Ella joins the now famed Jubilee Singers, and the musical group uses the college's entire treasury to travel through the South in a desperate—and success-ful—attempt to raise money for the school. Raúl Colón's dramatic illustrations, touched with gold, contribute elegance and warmth to this story. This unusual saga suggests how the actions of a few can benefit many, and it introduces a still-vibrant group whose performances are a delight to hear.

## Batman: Exploring the World of Bats

BY LAURENCE PRINGLE
PHOTOGRAPHS BY MERLIN D. TUTTLE
ATHENEUM, 1991. (U)

Ecologist Dr. Merlin Tuttle founded a society for the preservation of bats. By carefully document-ing bats' migratory habits and their niche in biodiversity, he almost single-handedly changed people's perceptions of bats as harmful and scary. This is a fascinating story, illustrated with Tuttle's own dramatic photographs of bats carrying their young, exiting their daytime lair by the thousands, and snagging insects out of the air. Like Pringle's other titles such as *Jackal Woman* (Atheneum, 1993), and *Scorpion Man* (Atheneum, 1994), this book shows how a person's passion can turn into an adult job. Diane Ackerman's lilting text for *Bats: Shadows of the Night* (Crown, 1997) features Tuttle's photographs and creates a sense of won-der while conveying information about bats for a slightly younger audience than Pringle's book. (Series)

## The Castle on Viola Street

BY DYANNE DISALVO
HARPERCOLLINS, 2001. (P, I)

Andy and his family work on a stranger's urban house renewal in order to earn the right to have others help them rehabilitate their own old house. This story introduces the idea of "Christmas in April" and similar programs while suggesting that communities change one piece at a time, drawing on the work of everyone. DiSalvo's previous book, (published under the author name of DiSalvo-Ryan), *Uncle Willie and the Soup Kitchen* (Morrow, 1997), features a child who volunteers with his uncle in a bustling urban soup kitchen. These are good stories for talking about community institu-tions, how they help and whom they benefit.

## Cool Crazy Crickets to the Rescue!

BY DAVID ELLIOTT
ILLUSTRATED BY PAUL MEISEL
CANDLEWICK, 2001. (I)

Four club members set up a series of moneymaking schemes to raise funds for treats for themselves. But a shabby, sick cat who hangs around their clubhouse needs help, so the group makes the magnanimous decision to spend their money on a veterinarian. In return, the veterinarian generously treats the cat for only $14 and the club gains a second mascot. This inviting early chapter book features realistic dialogue and a peek into the reasoning power of four eight-year-olds. Just as in Stephanie Greene's slightly more challenging *Owen Foote, Money Man*, in Chapter 1, there's also a subtle lesson about spending hard-earned money on something that matters. (Series)

## Edwina Victorious

BY SUSAN BONNERS
FARRAR, STRAUS & GIROUX, 2000. (U)

When Edwina discovers her great-grand Aunt Edwina's feisty letters to the editor, they give her the courage to write to the mayor about a neglected neighborhood playground and other civic blights. But young Edwina is too shy to write in her own voice so she adopts that of her aunt—with mixed consequences. This book introduces the concept of community activism, writing letters about things that need changing, and learning to speak up in your own voice. Ask children to write letters about changes they'd like to see in their own neighborhoods—and then mail them off and see what happens!

## Frank O. Gehry: Outside In

BY JAN GREENBERG AND SANDRA JORDAN
DK PUBLISHING, 2000. (U)

This photobiography shows how noted contemporary architect Frank O. Gehry has redefined what public buildings look like by using nontraditional materials and leaving electrical, water, and heating systems uncovered. The book's format and varied typefaces push the boundaries of conventional book making and set up interesting visual metaphors (a photograph of a bending Fred Astaire and Ginger Rogers faces a picture of Gehry's self-described "dancing building"). Readers and may be inspired to look at some of the buildings in their city or town and talk about their design and what makes them creative or boring. This can lead to discussion on the nature of artists and the way architecture and art can change the world.

## Hoot

BY CARL HIAASEN
KNOPF, 2002. (U)

Uprooted once again by his father's job, Roy Eberhardt has moved to southwest Florida and is the new kid in class. Roy misses the open spaces and mountains of his last home in Montana, the school bully taunts him by calling him "cowboy" and beats him up on the school bus, and life is pretty miserable. But then Roy gets involved in a campaign to save a wooded lot from commercial development and ends up coming to love his new home. Along the way, he manages to foil big business, garner support for endangered owls, and make friends in his new school. Quirky characters, exaggeration, and middle school humor are used to focus on one person's impact in changing both his personal and his natural environment. Many young readers will have their own preservation stories to share, as environmental issues are a topic children understand and care about from an early age.

## I Am Rosa Parks

BY ROSA PARKS WITH JIM HASKINS
ILLUSTRATED BY WIL CLAY
DIAL, 1997. (I)

In easy-to-read prose, this first-person narrative tells the story of the woman who became a beacon for the 1960s Civil Rights movement. When African-American Rosa Parks refused to give up her bus seat for a white traveler, as required by law, she sparked the successful Montgomery, Alabama, bus boycott. This victory galvanized activists across the nation, who ultimately persuaded the federal government to outlaw discrimination based on race. This autobiographical book is a good introduction to Rosa Parks and invites discussion of this era in which so many individual actions spurred others to join the struggle. Deborah Wiles' *Freedom Summer* for younger readers, in Chapter 3, and Christopher Paul Curtis' *The Watsons Go to Birmingham—1963*, in Chapter 1, present other aspects of this era in powerful, realistic fiction.

## The Jacket

BY ANDREW CLEMENT
ILLUSTRATED BY McDAVID HENDERSON
SIMON & SCHUSTER, 2002. (U)

In this brief, purposeful story, Phil is forced to examine his prejudices as a white boy when he mistakenly assumes that the jacket worn by Daniel, an African-American boy, has been stolen. The sixth grader painfully begins to notice the shallowness of his relationship with his beloved cleaning lady and his father's bigotry. Finally, he decides he must take action and makes his way through a tough neighborhood to apologize. Imagine his surprise when he gets to Daniel's middle class house and a wary friendship begins. The story forces readers to examine racial prejudice and suggests that everyone is responsible for eradicating it.

## Johnny Appleseed: The Story of a Legend

BY WILL MOSES
PHILOMEL, 2001. (I)

There are many versions of the story of John Chapman, who raised seedling apples and helped settlers throughout the central Midwest plant their homesteaded land with the government's required number of fruit trees. This one stays close to historical facts, marking the legends with "some say" to help readers see the real man and his ideas of generosity and simplicity, rather than the tall-tale version familiar to many children. Compare other *Johnny Appleseed* versions by Stephen Vincent Benet (illustrated by Stephen Schindler, McElderry, 2001), Steven Kellogg (Morrow, 1988), and Reeve Lindbergh (illustrated by Kathy Jakobson, Little, Brown, 1993), to name a few, and talk about content, tone, media, and adherence to facts.

## Judy Moody Saves the World

BY MEGAN MCDONALD
ILLUSTRATED BY PETER REYNOLDS
CANDLEWICK PRESS, 2002. (I)

Judy's third-grade class talks about small ways they can help save the world. Meanwhile, students study different endangered local species in their Virginia habitats. At home, Judy gets in trouble by going overboard with plans to recycle, hounding her family about their eating habits, and freeing her brother's pet toad. In a final insult, her broth-er's "batty" band-aid design wins a contest while Judy's mundane "heal the world" project doesn't. But she finishes strong when she spurs the class to conduct a recycling drive. This book will open discussions about ways to make your neighborhood better, even as it introduces a strong and humorous character. (Series)

## Making a Difference in the World

BY LYNNE CHERRY
RICHARD C. OWEN PUBLISHERS, 2000. (I)

Part of a "Meet the Author" series, this volume draws a link between a love of nature and children's literature. The author and illustrator of such environmentally conscious books as *The Great Kapok Tree* (Harcourt, 1990) and with Mark Plotkin, *The Shaman's Apprentice* (Harcourt, 1998), Cherry explains how her interest in preservation, ecology, and biodiversity turned into a career when she began creating children's books. Cherry advises writers to "pay attention to little things," but her impact has been large. Readers familiar with her fictionalized stories about endangered species and ecosystems will appreciate how children's book authors can use their work to change the way people look at the world. (Series)

## Martin's Big Words: The Life of Dr. Martin Luther King, Jr.

BY DOREEN RAPPAPORT
ILLUSTRATED BY BRYAN COLLIER
JUMP AT THE SUN, 2001. (P, I)

"When the history books are written, someone will say there lived black people who had the courage to stand up for their rights." Spare text and beautiful pictures combine with Dr. King's own powerful words to present a biographical tribute to the Civil Rights leader and his ideals. Brief biographical information leading up to and including his death is placed on each page with a quote from King in larger typeface. Children surely will want to talk about how the extraordinary mixed-media illustrations were made and why they so often resemble stained glass. This large-format volume is one of the best picture book biographies for introducing King and the Civil Rights era of the 1960s to younger children. Children will need some background to appreciate this book's scope, information that could be incorporated in your discussions.

## Mary On Horseback: Three Mountain Stories

BY ROSEMARY WELLS
ILLUSTRATED BY PETER MCCARTY
DIAL, 1998. (U)

Three moving fictional short stories, each introduced with McCarty's gentle pencil illustrations, give a glimpse of the work of an actual frontier nurse, Mary Breckenridge, in isolated Appalachia after World War I. A child seeks help for his father, who is injured in a logging accident; a timid Irish nurse who has never been out of the city courageously inoculates people against diphtheria; a small girl who has stopped talking after her mother dies finds her voice in helping Mary. Mary's enormous reserves of energy, her clear focus on what needed to be done, and her belief that courage came in many forms will inspire readers just as these admirable traits inspired her community years ago.

## Miss Rumphius

BY BARBARA COONEY
VIKING PENGUIN, 1982. (P, I)

In a look backward, a girl tells readers about her Great Aunt Alice. As a little girl, Alice wants to do three things: travel, live beside the sea, and do something to make the world more beautiful. As an adult in New England, Alice does all three, choosing to plant lupine flowers, with their purple blossoms climbing up a graceful stalk, as her act of beauty. The little girl who tells the story is encouraged by her great aunt to do her own something to make the world more beautiful. The book ends with her answer: "I do not know yet what that can be." This is a perfect discussion-starter of ways readers might beautify their own worlds.

## Out of Darkness: The Story of Louis Braille

BY RUSSELL FREEDMAN
ILLUSTRATED BY KATE KIESLER
CLARION, 1997. (I, U)

More than 175 years ago, a determined 15-year-old blind French boy, Louis Braille, invented a system of lettering that blind people could read with their fingertips. Louis Braille lost his sight at age three in an accident with a knife, but he never let his blindness slow him down. This short, readable biography includes diagrams of the Braille alphabet. It also gives readers a sense of the isolation and despair vision-impaired people felt when they couldn't read and were forced to depend on sighted people for access to information. Braille's persistence and flexibility in the face of setbacks is worth discussing.

## Passage to Freedom: The Sugihara Story

BY KEN MOCHIZUKI
ILLUSTRATED BY DOM LEE
LEE & LOW BOOKS, 1997. (I, U)

Hiroki Sugihara was only five years old when his father served as a Japanese diplomat in Lithuania. In 1940, when the Nazis invaded Poland, Jews poured into Lithuania, only to find themselves trapped. Despite his government's orders to the contrary, Hiroki's father wrote thousands of visas, from dawn to dusk for a month, allowing thousands of Jews to escape certain death by fleeing to Japan. This powerful story, told from Hiroki's point of view, is based on a true story and illustrates the immense reach of one person. Children will be especially anxious to discuss the role Hiroki plays in influencing his father to take action.

## Project UltraSwan

BY ELINOR OSBORN
HOUGHTON MIFFLIN, 2002. (I, U)

In a nonfiction photo-essay, Osborn details ongoing efforts of biologists to teach migration routes to endangered trumpeter swans who have been raised in outdoor labs by scientists disguised as birds. Unlike other birds, trumpeter swans learn migration from their parents. So the human surrogate "parents" in this book trained cygnets raised in Virginia to follow an ultralight aircraft along what would be their migratory route to the Atlantic coast. The scientists hoped to prompt these swans to return as adults and teach their young to migrate along the ultralight migratory path. Readers will be particularly fascinated to learn how biologists and scientists tinker with ideas and try one solution after another until something finally works. This book invites discussion about other endangered species and what people are doing to help preserve them. Like other books in the "Scientists in the Field" collection, it does a good job of portraying the qualities successful scientists must possess or cultivate. (Series)

## Ramona and Her Father

BY BEVERLY CLEARY
ILLUSTRATED BY ALAN TIEGREEN
WILLIAM MORROW, 1988. (I)

Energetic, stubborn, and thoroughly engaging, Ramona Quimby decides to start a campaign to get her father to stop smoking. But he's not ready to quit because he's feeling the stress of having lost his job and coping with Ramona's difficult older sister, Beezus. Ramona is a memorable, tenacious, and take-charge second grader whose schemes usually get results. Like Ramona, readers undoubtedly have also made plans to make life better for their families. Readers will have fun swapping stories of family improvement schemes—practical and not so practical. (Series)

## Seed Folks

BY PAUL FLEISCHMAN
HARPERCOLLINS, 1997. (U)

Hope sprouts from seeds planted in a blighted urban neighborhood by a girl grieving her father's death. One by one, others in the community see the growth of vegetables and flowers and add to the garden, creating a more beautiful and promising place. This slim novel is shaped by the distinct, individual voices of those who fashion the garden and change their community. Readers may know of other community garden projects or be interested in starting one. They may also notice that one event seen from multiple points of view has numerous outcomes, since all who participate in this garden are affected and changed in some way.

## Shades of Gray

BY CAROLYN REEDER
MACMILLAN, 1989. (U)

Following the death of his Yankee family from disease during the Civil War, bitter Will Paige must leave Winchester, Virginia, to live in the war-ravaged Shenandoah Valley with his uncle, a conscientious objector. Will thinks his uncle has chosen a coward's way, but Will must make some hard decisions, too, as he comes to see that choices aren't always black or white. Discuss the title, which is a metaphor for many aspects of the novel, and the reasons for Will's gradual change of mind as he sees the hardships in the Shenandoah Valley and realizes that this war changed many and benefited few. Reeder based details, such as a tiny basket carved from a peach pit by a wounded and bored soldier Will befriends, on her research in small museums near Civil War battle sites.

## Shiloh

BY PHYLLIS REYNOLDS NAYLOR
ATHENEUM, 1992. (U)

Marty sneaks a dog onto the family property, hides it in an upper field, and feeds it with food taken from his family's meager dinners. Though his actions in saving the dog he calls Shiloh were well-intentioned, Marty manages to infuriate just about everyone. As he works to regain his father's trust and pay off his debt to the dog's former owner, Judd Travers, Marty begins to understand some of the reasons for the man's angry and abusive behavior. Set in contemporary West Virginia, this book vividly portrays the family's rural mountain community. Encourage children to discuss what they think about Marty's decision to save Shiloh from his cruel owner and the other choices he makes as a consequence of his actions. (Series)

## The Signers: The Fifty-Six Stories Behind the Declaration of Independence

BY DENNIS FRADIN
ILLUSTRATED BY MICHAEL MCCURDY
WALKER, 2002. (U)

Brief but lively glimpses of the men who put their lives on the line to sign the Declaration of Independence are presented in 13 groups, one for each original colony. Fradin includes the usual well-known names (Thomas Jefferson, John Hancock, Benjamin Franklin) and some not-so-well-known (Richard Henry Lee, Steven Hopkins, and Joseph Hewes). These short biographies are introduced with information about each colony and accompanied by McCurdy's apt scratchboard illustrations, which look like rough etchings from Colonial hand-operated presses. Children will be delighted to discover why buildings, streets, or other places in their community bear the names of these famous men.

## Silver Packages: An Appalachian Christmas Story

BY CYNTHIA RYLANT
ILLUSTRATED BY CHRIS SOENTPIET
ORCHARD, 1997. (I)

In this fictional picture book, Frankie waits each year by the tracks near his Appalachian mining town for someone to toss him a present from the annual Christmas train. He always hopes for a play doctor's kit that never arrives but, as an adult, he returns to work as a doctor in the community that reared him. This is a perfect story for talking about ways we give back to those who help us become someone special. This story can also be found in Rylant's collection, *Children of Christmas* (Orchard, 1993). The real train, the "Santa Clause Special," still runs each year in late November, a project of the local Chamber of Commerce in Kingsport, Tennessee.

## Something Beautiful

BY SHARON DENIS WYETH
ILLUSTRATED BY CHRIS SOENTPIET
DOUBLEDAY, 1998. (P)

Saddened by the graffiti sprayed on her apartment building, the homeless person sleeping on the sidewalk, and the debris cluttering a vacant lot, a little girl searches for something beautiful. As she talks to people in the shops and on the street near her apartment, she gathers good feelings about her neighborhood and the people in it and begins to think of something she can do that's beautiful. Her mother rewards her by calling her beautiful inside, a sentiment echoed in Wyeth's personal note at the story's end. Compare this to Cooney's *Miss Rumphius* (above) to talk about "making the world a better place."

## The Story of Ruby Bridges

BY ROBERT COLES
ILLUSTRATED BY GEORGE FORD
SCHOLASTIC, 1995. (I)

First grader Ruby Bridges was the only attendee, black or white, in the Alabama elementary school that a judge ordered integrated in 1960. The six-year-old, accompanied by U.S. Marshals, bravely walked through hostile crowds to get an education, and gradually the white community, as well as the black, returned to school the following year. The image of a tiny black girl dressed in white flanked by enormous brown-suited men with armbands became famous across the country. This book introduces young children to a Civil Rights pioneer and invites children to talk about bravery.

## Talkin' About Bessie: The Story of Aviator Elizabeth Coleman

BY NIKKI GRIMES
ILLUSTRATED BY E.B. LEWIS
ORCHARD, 2002. (I, U)

Over a dozen different people make the past come alive when they share their memories of the life of the first licensed African-American pilot, Bessie Coleman. Striking watercolors and tiny sepia photograph-like circles of the speakers lend authenticity and warmth to this appealing, fictionalized, picture book biography. Readers are invited to think about Coleman's personality and the early 20th century during which she grew up. The book's format, which presents multiple points of view, also invites readers to discuss what is "true" in biography and what is speculation.

## They Called Her Molly Pitcher

BY ANNE ROCKWELL
ILLUSTRATED BY CYNTHIA VON BUHLER
KNOPF, 2002. (I)

In an era when women didn't do such things, Molly, an independent, loyal and strong woman, followed her husband to Valley Forge in 1777 and to the Battle of Monmouth the next summer. There she provided water to the thirsty soldiers ("Molly—pitcher!") and later took over firing a cannon when her husband was wounded. Not only does this picture book for older children present American Revolutionary historical background well, it also provides children with an opportunity to discuss how people do surprising but necessary things in hard times.

## Tomás and the Library Lady

BY PAT MORA
ILLUSTRATED BY RAÚL COLÓN
KNOPF, 1997. (P, I)

A child of a migrant farm family is changed forever by his visits to a library and his fleeting summer friendship with the librarian. This book is based on a true incident in the life of Mexican-American writer, Tomás Rivera, who went from being a farm laborer to serving as a chancellor in the California university system. Talking about Tomás will encourage kids to think about how librarians, books, and reading can change a person. A similar story is told in William Miller's book, *Richard Wright and the Library Card*, dramatically illustrated by Gregory Christie (Lee & Low, 1999).

## When My Name Was Keoko: A Novel of Korea in World War II

BY LINDA SUE PARK
CLARION, 2002. (U)

Ten-year-old Sun-hee and her older brother, Tae-yul, take turns telling stories in chapters that reveal the difficult lives they're leading under the Japanese occupation of Korea before and during World War II. As their Korean culture is nearly erased, the young people take pride in their family, though they fear losing their uncle, who is printing a resistance newspaper. Using her own family's experience, Park has fashioned a compelling and optimistic story about preserving family love, friendship, and trust in spite of hard times.

## William Shakespeare and the Globe

BY ALIKI
HARPERCOLLINS, 1998. (I, U)

The Globe Theatre serves as the stage for William Shakespeare, the playwright who made the Globe famous in Elizabethan England. This book tells of Shakespeare and of Sam Wanamaker, a 20th-century American actor and director who found financial backers and persuaded the British government to rebuild the open-air theater with its whitewashed, half-timbered walls and a thatched-roof crown. In this informative book, illustrations and text combine the stories of these men to reveal what creativity and dedication can achieve. While Shakespeare's plays have moved audiences for over four hundred years, Wanamaker's determination recreated an authentic site in which to see the plays performed. Older readers interested in this famous playwright will also enjoy Gary Blackwood's two exciting historical novels, *The Shakespeare Stealer* (1998) and *Shakespeare's Scribe* (2000, both Dutton). Those interested in Shakespeare, but not yet ready to read his plays, will enjoy Rebecca Piatt Davidson's *All the World's a Stage* (illustrated by Anita Lobel, Greenwillow, 2003).

## Yo! Yes?

BY CHRIS RASCHKA.
ORCHARD BOOKS, 1993. (P, I)

Something seemingly as simple as saying hello to another kid can make a big difference. In this book, one-syllable words in emotive typeface are integrated with expressive line drawings. Each is effectively placed on the page to depict two boys who are changed by a bold "YO!" Notice how the illustrations place the two boys on the pages in increasing closeness to mirror the wary characters' gradual friendship. Discuss how colors convey multiple meanings (e.g., the use of red connotes embarrassment as well as joy). But most of all, talk about how easy it is to start a friendship with a simple greeting.

# Chapter 10

# Exploring Imagination

*"Imagination is more important than knowledge. Knowledge is limited. Imagination encircles the world."*

Albert Einstein

Suppose clouds were created in a sky factory you could actually visit? What if you could really work magic, or travel back in time, or create your own civilization? What mischief might happen if characters stepped out of stories, subjects leaped off the canvas, or game pieces came alive? Such is the stuff of imagination.

Now, picture a world without imagination. There would be no history to study, no art to inspire, no stories to tell. Luckily, as long as there are children, there will be flights of fancy. Children instinctively know the power of creative thought. They like nothing better than to tinker around with objects, perhaps dismantle a new toy, try out a messy tube of paint, or, like the children in *Roxaboxen*, create a desert town of rocks, found objects, and tumbleweeds. Children naturally gravitate to the quixotic, the inventive, the curious. They don't find *Duck on a Bike* at all out of the ordinary, they would love to replicate *Milo's Hat Trick* and visit *The Garden of Abdul Gasazi*. Shout out, *Hey Kid, Want to Buy a Bridge?* and the answer is guaranteed to be "YES!" Some of the books we've listed here tell true stories of those whose creative insight and ingenuity changed the world. The hero in *The Dinosaurs of Waterhouse Hawkins* was the first to look at fossilized remains and reconstruct in three dimensions the creatures as they might have been. The inventors in *Girls Think of Everything: Stories of Ingenious Inventions by Women* gave us a host of highly practical everyday items that fascinated readers will recognize. And *How Ben Franklin Stole the Lightning* will satisfy the curiosity of any child who's ever wondered why buildings don't catch fire in the midst of electrical storms.

Other books we've selected encourage readers to change their point of view. An energetic mouse uses a variety of artistic expressions to cobble together his *Alphabet Under Construction*. *Two Bad Ants* offer a bug's-eye view of the kitchen, while *What's Up, What's Down* invites children to look at the world from the bottom up, until, halfway through, they turn the book around and start looking top down.

Some books in this chapter ask readers to think about the many ways that art can touch our lives—as inspirational beauty, as essential for community, as an outlet for emotions, or as something that speaks to others long after the creator has departed. A girl and her grandmother paint the walls of *Gugu's House* with vibrant patterns and charm the village. A continent away, in *The Pot That Juan Built*, a man living "on the windswept plains of Chihuahua" reclaims a lost art of making pottery. And artist Jackson Pollock, profiled in the gorgeous picture book biography *Action Jackson*, shocks and intrigues the art world with his vibrant abstract paintings.

# Outwitting My Own Wicked Witch

When I started school, I needed fairy tales as more than just magical escapes. Between first and third grade, I was diagnosed with dyslexia and ADHD, which made school very hard for me. I remember crying in the bathroom stalls because my friends had won blue and red ribbons for excellence in school. Then, on my 10th birthday, my mother read me this wonderful book by Rafe Martin called *The Rough-Face Girl*. This Algonquin Cinderella story depicts a girl ridiculed by her village for her burned and scarred appearance. But the Rough-Face Girl wins the love of the Invisible Being through faith in herself and a unique perspective on the world. I identified with an outsider who felt different from her peers, yet knew that she herself was special. The book didn't make my struggle any easier, but it helped me understand there were positive aspects to having a different perspective. Since then, I've cherished fairy tales differently. Learning about my own wicked witch—my disability—and how to outwit her remains one of my biggest accomplishments.

JANET DANIELS
STUDENT
MOUNT HOLYOKE COLLEGE
SOUTH HADLEY, MASSACHUSETTS

Books by gifted authors and illustrators invite us to imagine "what if...?" What if you went through *The Phantom Tollbooth* and found yourself in another world? What if *The Three Pigs* could walk outside the pages of their story? What if *Max Found Two Sticks*? What if poems were too weak to stand on the page and offered you *A Poke in the I*?

Whether it's a story about real or pretend characters who approach the world with imagination, or a story that plays catch with the imagination of the reader, books like these transport children to another universe and allow them to return refreshed, renewed, and perhaps with new ideas about how to look at life. The next time your kids ask "what-if" or wonder "what might happen," they'll know that just about anything is possible with a book!

**CHRIS RASCHKA'S** *illustrations and words play across the pages much like his favorite music, jazz. In fact, music often plays a key role in his imaginative work, such as* **Charlie Parker Played BeBop** *and* **John Coltrane's Giant Steps**. *Raschka's words and images engage even the youngest reader. His is a virtuoso performance on the page.*

**Music plays a strong role in your work. Even your images seem fluid and musical. Why does this play so strongly in your style?**

Because it challenges my skill and imagination to translate music to picture book imagery. I let the forms of music guide me in translating sounds to images. I do the same thing with words in concrete poetry. Both music and words can stretch your imagination and, in doing so, they open you up to even richer experiences.

# RECOMMENDED Books

P = PRIMARY (KINDERGARTEN – GRADE 3)
I = INTERMEDIATE (GRADE 3 – GRADE 4)
U = UPPER (GRADE 4 – GRADE 6)

## Action Jackson

BY JAN GREENBERG AND SANDRA JORDAN
ILLUSTRATED BY ROBERT ANDREW PARKER
ROARING BROOK PRESS, 2002. (I, U)

In this picture book biography, the authors imagine an afternoon in the life of painter Jackson Pollock. He called his paintings "energy and motion made visible" but people were shocked at Pollock's dribbled and thrown paint and his inclusion of dust, studio trash, and random insects that jumped onto his canvases. Pollock's work energized the art world and fueled the Abstract Expressionist movement. A short biographical note for older readers and fascinating source notes show the authors' extensive research. Readers can follow Jackson's fits and starts in the creative process and talk about how experimentation, frustration, and problem-solving figure in their own creative experiences.

## Alanna: The First Adventure

BY TAMARA PIERCE
ATHENEUM, 1983. (U)

Alanna and her twin brother look just alike but are different in every other way. Thor doesn't want to train as a knight, and Alanna doesn't want to be schooled in the convent; she rejects her magical abilities, he wants to better his. When they trade places, Alanna disguises herself as a boy and becomes a respected warrior dedicated to overcoming evil. Discussion may evolve around the "what-ifs" this adventurous fantasy presents, such as: What if Alanna had gone to the convent? What if she had not been successful in her quest? What if she had been discovered? (Series)

## Alphabet Under Construction

BY DENISE FLEMING
HENRY HOLT, 2002. (P)

Highly textured illustrations made with deeply dyed paper pulp give us the letters of the alphabet under construction by a toothy, engaging, energetic mouse. Note the lively verbs used to depict the mouse's work: he airbrushes, buttons, carves, etc. The alphabet has been used frequently to kindle imaginative thinking. For slightly older readers, Chris Van Allsburg's *The Z Was Zapped: The Alphabet in Twenty-Six Acts* (Houghton Mifflin, 1987) presents surreal, black and white depictions of each letter of the alphabet at a moment of great drama ("The A was in an avalanche"). Stephen Johnson's photo-realistic paintings in *Alphabet City* (Viking, 1996) see letters all over the urban landscape. Other mind-stretching alphabet books include Brad Sneed's *Picture a Letter* (Phyllis Fogelman Books/Penguin Putnam, 2002) and *Alphabatics* by Suse MacDonald (Simon & Schuster, 1986).

## And to Think That I Saw It on Mulberry Street

BY DR. SEUSS
RANDOM HOUSE, 1989 (1937). (P, I)

Marco has been instructed by his father to report the remarkable things he sees on the way to school. Somehow, a plain old-fashioned horse-drawn carriage becomes "a story no one can beat/And to think that I saw it on Mulberry Street" when Marco's imagination kicks in. A magician with a long beard? A reindeer and sleigh! No, a blue elephant with a Rajah to pull the sleigh! The story grows wilder and crazier— that is, until Marco faces his stern father. Turned down by over 20 publishers on the way to becoming a beloved classic, this rhythmic story, with wonderful wordplay and Seuss's curvy, energetic cartoons, is great fun to read aloud. Seuss steadfastly maintained that his books were for fun, not for moralizing, and this early Dr. Seuss book is one of his most entertaining.

## The Birdwatchers

### BY SIMON JAMES
CANDLEWICK, 2002. (P)

Jess can't resist her grandfather's tall stories: "I got all the birds together one morning to record the dawn chorus, just for you," and "Sometimes the birds help me when I can't find their names in my bird book." Jess goes birdwatching with her grandfather. At first she can't figure out the binoculars and can't find any birds either. But once she climbs into the "birdwatching hut" and sees yellow warblers, ducks, herons, and all sorts of other birds, she's a convert, not only to bird-watching, but also to her grandfather's inventive exaggerations. Says Jess, "I liked it best when the dancing penguins came and shared my sandwich." Compare other grandfatherly exaggerated humor in the James Stevenson series that begins with *Could Be Worse!"* (Greenwillow, 1977).

## Black and White

### BY DAVID MACAULAY
HOUGHTON MIFFLIN, 1990. (I, U)

Does this book contain one story or four different ones about commuters waiting for a train, a jailbreaker, a wacky family that makes clothes out of newspapers, and some cows? Macaulay opens with a warning note that, "This book appears to contain a number of stories that do not necessarily occur at the same time. Then again, it may contain only one story. In any event, careful inspection of both words and pictures is recommended." Double pages are divided into four seemingly separate stories that gradually blend into each other. Characters show up in each other's quadrants, the jailbreaker is camouflaged by the cows, bored commuters decorate themselves in newspapers, and a hand mysteriously appears at the end. The ingenious book design begs readers to talk about what is happening. Get multiple copies and let small groups of children explore this energetic book. They'll all come up with different interpretations.

## Book

### BY GEORGE ELLA LYON
ILLUSTRATED BY PETER CATALANOTTO
DK, 1999. (P, I)

"A BOOK is a HOUSE/that is all windows and doors." With these lines, readers are invited to celebrate the joys found between the covers of books. The simple, poetic text may generate discussion of different types of books—fantasy, real stories, and more—as well as the imaginative pleasures found in books. Illustrations in luminous watercolors show what a reader imagines as she pores over books. A natural follow-up is to let children re-sort their own library (in the classroom or at home) according to their own categories.

## The Dinosaurs of Waterhouse Hawkins

### BY BARBARA KERLEY
ILLUSTRATED BY BRIAN SELZNICK
SCHOLASTIC, 2001. (I, U)

No one knew what a dinosaur looked like until Victorian artist and showman Waterhouse Hawkins created full-scale models by imagining muscle, bone, and spike from fossil remains. He reasoned that if a fossil tooth resembled an iguana's, then the resulting dinosaur would look like a giant iguana. He built models on brick foundations with iron skeletons covered with cement and toured London and New York lecturing about these ancient animals. One illustration compares Hawkins' rendition of Iguanadon and four other dinosaur types as we render them now. While Hawkins may have been wrong in some of his imagined shapes, his efforts stretched the boundaries of what had been known of dinosaurs. Brilliant author and illustrator notes reveal Kerley's inspiration and research while Selznick recounts his magical discovery of Hawkins' original drawings and what remains of the models.

## Duck on a Bike

BY DAVID SHANNON
BLUE SKY PRESS, 2002. (P)

What happens when Duck gets a wild idea to try to ride a bike? All the other animals criticize him, saying bicycles are silly, dangerous, boring, and slow. But when some boys park their bikes by the farmhouse, every animal takes a ride. Then, it's, "Good idea, Duck!" This funny story is sure to inspire talk about what happens when one person invents or tries something new. The last page offers a tantalizing invitation for readers to predict or write about what's going to happen next as duck contemplates a shiny red tractor.

## Ella Enchanted

BY GAIL CARLSON LEVINE
HARPERCOLLINS, 1997. (U)

A fairy bestows upon Ella at birth the "gift of obedience," which ironically makes Ella want to rebel—especially after her mother's death when she's left with her avaricious father, a nasty stepmother, and equally nasty stepsisters. What emerges is a plucky heroine, a new take on a familiar tale, and a satisfying conclusion. Not only is Ella's point of view worth exploring, so are the different motives of her stepfamily and her growing relationship with a prince. This book pairs well with Laura Whipple's *If the Shoe Fits* (also in this chapter) for further discussion of perspective and what happens when a fairy tale is retold from a different character's point of view. More sophisticated readers may want to discuss Donna Jo Napoli's *Zel* (Dutton, 1996), the story of Rapunzel told from three distinct points of view, including that of the witch.

## Galimoto

BY KAREN LYNN WILLIAMS
ILLUSTRATED BY CATHERINE STOCK
LOTHROP, LEE & SHEPARD, 1990. (P, I)

Kondi wants to build a *galimoto*, a wheeled wire toy on the end of a steering stick. He uses his own supplies, bargains with a little girl for a length of wire, finds other wire pieces at a bicycle repair shop, and finally assembles this national toy of Malawi. The busy life of an African village makes an informative backdrop as Kondi creatively uses what is at hand to make his truck. Children might locate Malawi on a map and note how Stock's illustrations show natural details of this lakeside village. Readers might also enjoy talking about toys they've made or, like Kondi, scrounge wire from their neighborhoods and make a *galimoto*.

## The Garden of Abdul Gasazi

BY CHRIS VAN ALLSBURG
HOUGHTON MIFFLIN, 1979. (I)

Alan agrees to watch Miss Hester's unruly dog Fritz, but Fritz runs away to the forbidden garden of the magician, Abdul Gasazi. When Alan timidly approaches Gasazi about returning Fritz, the magician informs him that he turns garden-digging dogs into ducks and only time will turn the magic around. Gasazi gives him the duck who was formerly Fritz. But the duck flies off with Alan's hat and Alan must confess what has happened to Miss Hester. But then Fritz appears. Was he really turned into a duck? Perhaps the hat holds a clue. Children can sift the evidence to decide whether there's magic involved or not. Read Van Allsburg's books in chronological order to see how an author/illustrator plays with magic and the reader's imagination, repeats the dog Fritz in the pictures, changes from black and white artwork to full color, and continues to explore point of view.

## The Gawgon and the Boy

BY LLOYD ALEXANDER
DUTTON, 2001. (U)

While recuperating from near-fatal pneumonia, 11-year-old David is forced to accept tutoring from an elderly aunt. She turns out to be just the right teacher for the boy as she encourages his imagination and introduces him to literary and mythical characters. The novel's setting, Philadelphia in the 1920s, is worth discussing. David's discovery of the new "talkie" movies may prompt readers to compare notes about this book and Avi's *Silent Movie* (covered later in this chapter). Also worth discussing is the way the author introduces and explores the personalities of various characters and the role of imagination in David's recovery.

## Girls Think of Everything: Stories of Ingenious Inventions by Women

BY CATHERINE THIMMESH
ILLUSTRATED BY MELISSA SWEET
HOUGHTON MIFFLIN, 2000. (I, U)

How on earth did someone think of Velcro®? Where did the idea for the 'Snugli' baby carrier, Wite-Out, Kevlar, Scotchgard, windshield wipers and other common inventions come from? From little-known but important women inventors, profiled in some dozen sketches in this book. The sketches include anecdotes, dialogue and quotes, clever collage-like paintings, and an invitation to both boys and girls to "take your turn" and think of inventions we need. The author and illustrator present other inventions in *The Sky's the Limit: Stories of Discovery by Women and Girls* (Houghton Mifflin, 2002).

## Gooney Bird Greene

BY LOIS LOWRY
ILLUSTRATED BY MIDDY CHILMAN THOMAS
HOUGHTON MIFFLIN, 2002. (I)

An eccentric second-grade girl, who really is named Gooney Bird, arrives at school and turns out to be a dynamic storyteller. She tells tales about herself that sound incredible, like driving from China or flying on a carpet. But they all turn out to be true. Lowry uses Gooney Bird's patient second-grade teacher to remind readers about what comprises a good story and to inspire children to tell their own family stories. Older readers will appreciate Lowry's humor and enjoy looking back on the sometimes exasperating behavior of second graders.

## Gugu's House

BY CATHERINE STOCK
CLARION, 2001. (P, I)

Kukamba visits her artist grandmother in Zimbabwe, where they entertain themselves by painting murals on the walls and courtyard of their village compound. In the evening, when everyone gathers to escape the heat and listen to stories, the artwork disappears in the darkness. And it disappears forever when the rains finally come. But Kukamba sees the colors coming back on the greening landscape. Children might discuss different kinds of artistic expression and how art benefits people. Older readers might discuss whether art, like the stories grandmother tells or the walls she paints, must be permanent in order to be authentic.

## Hey Kid, Want to Buy a Bridge?

BY JON SCIESZKA
ILLUSTRATED BY ADAM MCCAULEY
VIKING, 2002. (I)

The "Time Warp Trio" uses "The Book" and ends up in Brooklyn in 1877 before the bridge has been built. There they meet young Thomas Edison, who may or may not go on to do great things, and encounter their own great-granddaughters, who have been doing some time-slip travel of their own. This imaginative series treats history lightly with short, punchy chapters and plenty of broad humor sure to propel even the most reluctant readers through the story as they guess how the boys will get back to their own time. (Series)

## How Ben Franklin Stole the Lightning

BY ROSALYN SCHANZER
HARPERCOLLINS, 2003. (I, U)

Each of Benjamin Franklin's many accomplishments—ranging from music, to writing, and even politics—required quick thinking. But perhaps his greatest strength was the ability to "come up with newfangled ways to help folks out." In the 1750s, he started wondering how to keep buildings from catching fire when they were struck by lightning. He finally figured out a way to guide lightning's "electric fire" down metal rods from the rooftop to the ground, which led to the invention of lightning rods. Lively illustrations complement informal text in this glimpse into Franklin's life and work; an afterword supplies more biographical information.

## If the Shoe Fits: Voices from Cinderella

BY LAURA WHIPPLE
ILLUSTRATED BY LAURA BEINGESSNER
MCELDERRY, 2002. (I, U)

A now "old and quiet" Cinderella, "content with memories," provides the first look at an old tale in this collection of poems told from unusual points of view. Readers learn why Cinderella's father married and of the greed that motivated his new wife. Even inanimate objects, like each of

Cinderella's glass slippers, have their say. The different voices are sometimes humorous, sometimes serious, often surprising, and may generate interest in exploring familiar stories from new directions.

## Little Lit: Folklore & Fairy Tale Funnies

EDITED BY ART SPIEGELMAN AND FRANÇOISE MOULY
JOANNA COTLER/HARPERCOLLINS, 2000. (I, U)

This imaginative use of comic book format should captivate not only reluctant readers but also would-be cartoon artists. Like graphic novels popular with middle-school and high-school readers, these cartooned stories play with a variety of line, color, form, and storytelling techniques that go beyond a simple comic book. Compare one of the folktales here, such as Walt Kelly's treatment of "The Gingerbread Man," with picture book versions and talk about the strengths and appeals of each format. Children could interview a grownup to see what he or she thinks about comics and why. The editors have also assembled *Little Lit: Strange Stories for Strange Kids* (2001) and *Little Lit: It Was a Dark and Silly Night* (2003, both HarperCollins).

## Lizards, Frogs, and Polliwogs: Poems and Paintings

BY DOUG FLORIAN
HARCOURT, 2001. (P, I, U)

Twenty-one short, humorous poems in a variety of shapes use antic wordplay, internal rhyme, surprisingly apt comparisons, and humor to grab readers' and writers' attention. As in his *Insectlopedia* (1998), *Mammalabelia* (2000), and *Summersaults* (2002, all Harcourt), Florian gives children a new and entirely fresh way of looking at common actions and animals. Arresting illustrations on brown bag paper should inspire readers to experiment with the medium. The more you know about reptiles, insects, and animals, the more you can appreciate the wealth of information Florian slyly presents with such an economy of word and art.

## Maker of Things

BY DENISE FLEMING
RICHARD C. OWEN, 2002. (I)

Ohio-born picture book creator Denise Fleming tells readers how she grew up drawing and observing nature, two pleasures she combined to become an author/illustrator. Her picture books include *In a Small, Small Pond* (1993) and *In the Tall, Tall Grass* (1991, both Holt). The ecological messages of her books and the craft of her artwork can be appreciated by children as young as second grade. Photos from Fleming's childhood and from her present life show the mess of notes and drafts she needs to write her stories. Readers also get a glimpse of the organized chaos in her art studio, where she creates imaginative handmade paper illustrations by pouring colored paper pulp through stencils onto screens. Fleming provides enough information on this technique to allow readers armed with a blender and some paint to experiment with this medium. (Series)

## Max Found Two Sticks

BY BRIAN PINKNEY
SIMON & SCHUSTER, 1994. (P)

Max likes to make rhythms inside his head and imagine he's a drummer. When he finds two sticks, he drums out rhythms on all sorts of objects he can reach from his front steps. Max makes the rhythm of *putter-putter, pat-tat* for the sounds of pigeon flight and *cling, clang, da-bang* for train sounds. It's a sure bet that readers will imitate Max and try to capture the sounds they hear every day. The author renders the details of Max's urban neighborhood by using energetic scratchboard illustrations, a technique of scraping lines in black-inked paper that children can also easily imitate. A story of another boy whose love of rhythm earns him drumsticks can be found in Colby Rodowsky's novel for older children, *Jason Rat-a-Tat,* in Chapter 6.

## Milo's Hat Trick

BY JON AGEE
HYPERION, 2001. (P)

Milo the magician is not very successful until he hires a bear and tells him to just pretend his bones are rubber and jump into the black hat. The two perform happily until the bear grows tired of jumping into hats and takes a break. Readers will be surprised and delighted when Milo disappears into the hat. How the seemingly simple illustrations move the story along is worth talking about, as is Milo's magic, which may generate disagreement as to whether it's real or imagined.

## Nothing Ever Happens on 90th Street

BY RONI SCHOTTER
ILLUSTRATED BY KYRSTEN BROOKER
ORCHARD BOOKS, 1997. (I)

Eva is sitting on the stoop of her apartment house, stumped about what to write for a school paper. Neighbors, as they pass by, throw her suggestions as wide ranging and diverse as the fascinating neighborhood she sees from her front steps. Inspired by a ballerina's advice to "Stretch. Use your imagination....You can ask 'What if?'" Eva sets her imagination free—with some interesting consequences for 90th Street. Illustrations incorporating scraps of newspaper, patterned cloth, and other bits and pieces of found objects give readers a lovely feel for Eva's world. Lisa Broadie Cook's *The Author on My Street* (R.C. Owen, 2000) features a literal-minded girl and an imaginative author talking about things they see in terms of their story possibilities; Marc Brown's *Arthur Writes a Story* (Little Brown, 1996) shows how "writing about what you know" can easily be as creative as make-believe plotlines. Books such as this help children discuss where to find writing ideas and how to overcome writer's block.

## Olivia Joins the Circus

BY IAN FALCONER
ANNE SCHWARTZ/ATHENEUM, 2001. (P)

At school, the irrepressible Olivia volunteers to tell about her vacation. Always at her best in front of an audience, she invents a fine day at the circus in which she had to take the place of all the performers, who were suddenly been stricken with ear infections. Notice how the artwork changes subtly as Olivia's imagination takes over. Falconer first introduced this wildly imaginative character in *Olivia* (2000).

## The Phantom Tollbooth

BY NORTON JUSTER
ILLUSTRATED BY JULES FEIFFER
RANDOM HOUSE, 1961. (U)

When a bored Milo goes through a peculiar tollbooth in this modern classic, he discovers a land in which mathematicians are warring with wordsmiths and the geography includes the Foothills of Confusion, the Sea of Knowledge, a ticking watchdog called Tock, and the city of Dictionopolis. Wordplay, jokes, puns, and sly allusions should appeal to children with some prior academic knowledge. Readers will enjoy talking about what's funny and why, as well as how authors and illustrators use different sorts of humor.

## A Poke in the I: A Collection of Concrete Poems

SELECTED BY PAUL JANECZKO
ILLUSTRATED BY CHRIS RASCHKA
CANDLEWICK, 2001. (I, U)

The spectacular possibilities of visual poetry ripple through this imaginative collection of concrete poems. There's a "weak poem" that can hardly stand up straight on the page, a poem about tennis that has readers swiveling their heads, and a letter hiding in the center of the poem "STOWaWAY." This is the sort of book that makes readers grin when they see what the poet has accomplished. Children will surely be challenged to try creating their own concrete poems.

## The Pot That Juan Built

BY NANCY ANDREWS-GOEBEL
ILLUSTRATED BY DAVID DIAZ
LEE & LOW, 2002. (P, I)

When Juan Quezada and his family moved to Mata Ortiz, a village on the "windswept plains of Chihuahua," he rediscovers a process used to create distinctive pottery that was lost to the region centuries earlier. Stylized illustrations incorporate patterns and motifs used in this traditional art form, while introducing the artist and his impact on his village. Younger readers might talk about how to make a pot and how an artistic technique can be lost and then found. Older readers might examine the role of art in a community and why traditional art forms resonate so strongly with contemporary audiences.

## Roxaboxen

BY ALICE MCLAREN
ILLUSTRATED BY BARBARA COONEY
LOTHROP, 1991. (P, I)

The author remembers the real-life Arizona hillside "town" her mother and others created on the sandy desert from found objects: rocks, greasewood, bits of sun-crazed glass, ocotillo cactus wands, and boxes. There they played in the stone-outlined imaginary stores, houses, jails, town halls, and schools or galloped about with pretend horses made of sticks and string bridles. Cooney's glowing hues capture the subtle colors of the desert and the town's dimensions. Readers will want to talk about their own settings, forts, or play areas created from whatever objects they could find and about the games they play there. Imaginative builders may want to find an out-of-the-way corner and create their own "Roxaboxen."

## Sector 7

BY DAVID WEISNER
CLARION BOOKS, 1999. (P)

This eloquent story uses only pictures to tell of a boy's field trip to the Empire State building that evolves into a journey to the place in the sky where clouds are assembled and released. Readers will need to make several trips through the pictures to tell the story well and decipher intriguing clues to the emotions of the different sky characters the boy meets. As in many of Chris Van Allsburg's books, Wiesner's boy has exuberant evidence by the story's end that his adventure really happened and wasn't just a dream. Small groups of children may take turns telling the story and pointing out visual clues and surprises. And, of course, the friendly cloud, the boy, the annoyed cloud foreman, or the puzzled adult might all tell the story from their own points of view.

## Silent Movie

BY AVI
ILLUSTRATED BY C.B. MORDAN
ANNE SCHWARTZ/ATHENEUM, 2003. (I, U)

Children (and many adults) may have difficulty believing that movies once had no sound and were in black and white only. This carefully crafted book helps readers visualize the tension and intrigue of the silent movie era as they witness the dramatic story of an immigrant family separated then reunited and of the son who foils the villain and becomes the star of silent film. Discuss how this clever book captures a bygone era and the role of imagination in making and watching old films.

## The Three Pigs

BY DAVID WEISNER
CLARION BOOKS, 2001. (P, I)

The three pigs slip from the confines of the printed page and find another world outside their story. There they meet the cat and the fiddle, the cow that jumped over the moon, and a knight-pursued dragon all searching for another more peaceful story in which to reside. Wiesner's art style changes for each story type, and the white space becomes an important part of the visual design. Like David Macaulay's *Black and White* (earlier in this chapter), this story demands that active readers talk about what is really happening and what the pictures reveal that the text doesn't. Readers will enjoy seeing how the pigs and dragon images included in Wiesner's wordless first book, *Free Fall* (Lothrop, 1988) play a central role here.

## Two Bad Ants

BY CHRIS VAN ALLSBURG
HOUGHTON MIFFLIN, 1988. (P, I)

With illustrations that let readers see the kitchen from a bug's vantage point, Van Allsburg presents the story of ants who leave their colony looking for more of a delicious crystal brought home by a fellow ant. Van Allsburg describes the adventures the two disobedient ants have in ant-perspective text—they fall into a lake that disappears into a pitch black hole (coffee being drunk by a man) and find themselves whirring in a storm of food (being caught in the garbage disposal). Readers will enjoy the contrast between deadpan narrative written from an ant's point of view and pictures showing how the action plays out in a human kitchen. Like other titles in this chapter, explore how point of view changes the way readers perceive the facts of a story.

## Weslandia

BY PAUL FLEISCHMAN
ILLUSTRATED BY KEVIN HAWKES
CANDLEWICK, 1999. (I)

Bored with the usual silly summer activities, Wesley decides to plan and create his own civilization. From the fruits of an exotic plant that mysteriously grows in his garden, he constructs a dwelling, makes clothes, and feeds himself. For the new civilization he invents noncompetitive games, a unique number system, and a new language. His efforts attract other bored students from his school, who engage in the life of Weslandia, and the formerly distained Wesley has plenty of friends when he returns to school in the fall. The book invites readers to talk about ways they combat boredom and imagine what they might do to fill a summer without camp, television, video games, and the sort of organized activities that involve uniforms, memberships, or entrance fees.

## What's Up, What's Down

BY LOLA M. SCHAEFER
ILLUSTRATED BY BARBARA BASH
GREENWILLOW, 2002. (P)

By turning the book sideways, readers will see the earth from a mole's eye-view—up through the grass, past animals, flowers, trees, butterflies, birds, and finally to the sky. Halfway through, by turning the book around, readers will discover animals and plants from high in the sky—starting with clouds, to ocean waves, through the water, to the bottom of the sea. Poetic text and the orderly bottom-to-top-to-bottom approach encourage young children to think about layers of nature and what they might contain. Schaefer also expertly introduces the concept of cross-sections and cutaways. In *Looking Down* (Houghton Mifflin, 1995), Steve Jenkins zooms in from outer space and, picture by picture, gradually closes in on a boy looking at a bug. In *Zoom* (Viking, 1995), Istvan Banya moves out from a farm, to a boat, to a town, and, with each jump away, readers are challenged to reexamine their assumptions. Books such as these should entice children into lying on the ground to talk about what they see by looking up or looking down.

## Who Was the Woman Who Wore the Hat?

BY NANCY PATZ
DUTTON, 2003. (U)

After seeing a hat in the Jewish Historical Museum in Amsterdam, the author/illustrator began to imagine who owned it, when she wore it, who else she might have known, and if the hat was the only remnant of her life. Patz combines sparse, poetic text with collage illustrations of pencil drawings and actual photographs in this seemingly simple book. Readers will wonder, muse, and imagine how one person might have been caught in the atrocities of the Holocaust. They also might unleash their own imaginations to create a life for the owner of a family artifact or historical item. An informational book with a similar approach for younger readers is *Hana's Suitcase: A True Story* by Karen Levine (Albert Whitman, 2003). Here students studying the Holocaust track the mystery inspired by a suitcase they see during a museum visit in Japan.

# Tools & Techniques

Whether you're in the classroom, family room, or clubroom, the tools in this section will help you make the most of the time you spend reading with children. You'll find a variety of tips and strategies to help children further explore the ideas raised in each chapter. Of course, each chapter already contains many talking ideas specific to each book title. Here, we suggest ways children can move into other areas of the topic, learn from other resources about the topic, and keep on thinking and talking. We've included activities that take into account children's learning styles and different degrees of comfort with various kinds of projects: arts and crafts, community involvement, research, group or individual projects, interviews, movement or dance, writing skills, and more. Some activities identify and group two or more book titles that offer good comparisons or feature other similarities.

Each section begins with some key questions that can help you frame discussion of the main chapter topic. The questions are followed by notes about some of the many other themes raised by the books in that chapter. We then suggest activities, extensions, and experiences for adults to use as tools with young readers. You'll see that most of the "ideas to get you started" are addressed to children. This saves you time in trying to rephrase ideas to convey to a child. Each section ends with a list of books from other chapters that are also related to the topic we're discussing.

## Classroom and Family Treasures

Remember that one child's activity is fine all by itself. Several children's activities make a party, a presentation for someone else, or a great display. One child's writing is a family treasure. Several children's writings reprinted and bound together make a memorable class book, a wonderful book for rereading, or a cherished present reproduced for every family to share.

## CHAPTER 1: Living in a Family

*What is a family? How do families show they care for each other?*
The books in this chapter present diverse families in many con-figurations. Each family has certain strengths or supports its members in different ways. We think conversations about these books might center on the following themes: families have various make-ups; accepting family members; the value of family history, memories, and stories; the multiple roles of stories in a family's life; accepting and cherishing elders; the importance of birth order in a family; family celebrations; connecting to our ancestors and previous generations; activities families do together.

*Some ideas to get you started:*

• Read a book, such as *Cherry Pies and Lullabies* or *Dim Sum for Everyone*, and talk about favorite or special foods in your own family. Make or take a picture of your family enjoying those foods, or create a group recipe book of favorite foods. Families might get together for a potluck of favorite dishes, and children could help cook and make fancy labels for each dish.

• Invite an older person who grew up in a very large family, a different country, a different area from the one in which you live, or who has lived in your area for a long time to talk about his or her childhood. Before you invite the person to talk with you, write down some questions, such as "How did your family celebrate birthdays?" or "What kind of chores did you have?" to get started.

• Imagine you joined the family in one of the books in this chapter. Where would you fit in? What would you do with the children in that book? Write a story about your visit or talk with someone about your life with that family.

• Look at some of the books on this list that are based on true family stories, such as *Potato: A Tale from the Great Depression; Tell Me A Story, Mama; Seven Brave Women;* and *Aunt Flossie's Hats (and Crab Cakes Later)*. Then, tell your own story about something that has happened to you in your family, or draw a picture of a favorite family story.

• Interview your oldest family members about their childhoods. What did they do for fun? How did they spend their summers? What were their favorite foods, games, books, movies, sports? Did they listen to the radio or have favorite television shows? What was a school day like for them?

• Make a scrapbook of houses you'd like to live in, as Maddie did in *Where I'd Like to Be*. You could draw the houses or cut them out of magazines. Perhaps it's the house you live in now. Use markers or crayon to make your picture lively. Then write or tell about features of your house that are special to you.

**Books in other chapters that also explore the themes of Living in a Family:**

*Amber Was Brave, Essie Was Smart* by Vera B. Williams. Chap. 8 (I)

*Anastasia Krupnik* by Lois Lowry. Chap. 6 (U)

*Angel Spreads Her Wings* by Judy Delton. Chap. 6 (I)

*Apple Pie 4th of July* by Janet Wong. Chap. 5 (P)

*The Ballad of Lucy Whipple* by Karen Cushman. Chap. 4 (U)

*Brave as a Mountain Lion* by Ann Herbert Scott. Chap. 2 (P, I)

*Bridge to Terebithia* by Katherine Paterson. Chap. 3 (U)

*Bud, Not Buddy* by Christopher Paul Curtis. Chap. 6 (U)

*The Castle on Viola Street* by Dyanne DiSalvo. Chap. 9 (P, I)

*Chang and the Bamboo Flute* by Elizabeth Starr Hill. Chap. 6 (I)

*Celebrating Ramadan* by Diane Hoyt-Goldsmith. Chap. 5 (I)

*Child of the Owl* by Laurence Yep. Chap. 4 (U)

*Deshawn Days* by Tony Medina. Chap. 4 (I, U)

*Dream Carver* by Diana Cohn. Chap. 6 (I)

*Double Fudge* by Judy Blume. Chap. 7 (I, U)

*Edwina Victorious* by Susan Bonners. Chap. 9 (U)

*Escaping to America: A True Story* by Rosalyn Schanzer. Chap. 4 (I)

*Esperanza Rising* by Pam Muñoz Ryan. Chap. 4 (U)

*Families* by Ann Morris. Chap. 5 (P)

*Flamingo Dream* by Donna Jo Napoli. Chap. 8 (P, I)

*Gershon's Monster* by Eric Kimmel. Chap. 8 (I)

*Grandmother Bryant's Pocket* by Jacqueline Briggs Martin. Chap. 8 (I)

*Gus and Grandpa and the Christmas Cookies* by Claudia Mills. Chap. 4 (P)

*Home at Last* by Susan Middletown Elya. Chap. 5 (P, I)

*Hoot* by Carl Hiaasen. Chap. 9 (U)

*How My Parents Learned to Eat* by Ina Friedman. Chap. 5 (P)

*Jason Rat-a-Tat* by Colby Rodowsky. Chap. 6 (I)

*Journey to an 800 Number* by E.L. Konigsburg. Chap. 6 (U)

*Just Juice* by Karen Hesse. Chap. 8 (U)

*Marianthe's Story: Painted Words/Spoken Memories* by Aliki. Chap. 2 (P, I, U)

*Marvin One Too Many* by Katherine Paterson. Chap. 2 (P, I)

*Max* by Bob Graham. Chap. 6 (P)

*Mick Harte Was Here* by Barbara Park. Chap. 6 (U)

*The Most Beautiful Place in the World* by Ann Cameron. Chap. 5 (I, U)

*My Louisiana Sky* by Kimberly Willis Holt. Chap. 3 (U)

*Nadia's Hands* by Karen English. Chap. 5 (I)

*Not My Dog* by Colby Rodowsky. Chap. 6 (I)

*Once Upon a Time* by Niki Daly. Chap. 8 (P)

*Other Side of Truth* by Beverly Naidoo. Chap. 5 (U)

*Owen Foote, Money Man* by Stephanie Greene. Chap. 1 (I)

*Pictures of Hollis Woods* by Patricia Giff Reilly. Chap. 8 (U)

*Potato: A Tale from the Great Depression* by Kate Lied. Chap. 8 (P, I)

*Powwow* by George Ancona. Chap. 4 (I)

*Ramona and Her Father* by Beverly Cleary. Chap. 9 (I)

*Ramona Quimby, Age 8* by Beverly Cleary. Chap. 6 (I)

*Ruby's Wish* by Shirin Yim Bridges. Chap. 2 (I)

*7 X 9 = Trouble* by Claudia Mills. Chap. 2 (I, U)

*Skinnybones* by Barbara Park. Chap. 7 (I, U)

*Snake Charmer* by Ann Whitehead Nagda. Chap. 5 (I)

*The Steps* by Rachel Cohn. Chap. 8 (U)

*Storm Warriors* by Elisa Carbone. Chap. 6 (U)

*The Talent Show* by Michelle Edwards. Chap. 2 (I)

*Three Cheers for Catherine the Great* by Cari Best. Chap. 4 (P)

*Trout and Me* by Susan Shreve. Chap. 3 (U)

*Uncle Jed's Barbershop* by Margaree King Mitchell. Chap. 4 (I)

*Visiting Day* by Jacqueline Woodson. Chap. 8 (P, I)

*Willow and Twig* by Jean Little. Chap. 8. (U)

## CHAPTER 2: Going to School

*What happens in school? How do people make friends and solve problems there?*

The books in this chapter present a wide variety of school experiences that draw on themes such as: becoming a successful student; making friends; handling strong personalities or bullies; the positive impact of a memorable teacher; being different or just being yourself; facing challenging subject matter successfully; going to school in another country or culture.

*Some ideas to get you started:*

• Read a few books about the first days of school, such as *Elizabeti's School, First Graders from Mars: Horus's Horrible Day,* or *The Name Jar.* Talk about first-day jitters, and remember your own first days in a particular school or classroom. Interview an older person to see what he remembers about his first days in school. Ask a former teacher about her first days of teaching school.

• What school subject are you good in right now? In what kind of jobs would these skills be needed? Draw a two-part before/after picture split down the middle, with one side showing you working at this subject in school and the other side showing you grown up and working at a job related to this subject.

• Invite someone who used to live in another country to talk about what going to school was like for them. Prepare a few questions, such as: How did you get to school? What subjects did you study? What were your teachers like? What games did you play for recess? What were lunches like? Did you have to wear special uniforms?

• Make a map of your classroom or a floor plan of your school. Note important places and what you do there, what you like about that place, or why it's important. You could include a map key.

• Adopt a school in some other part of the country or in another country. Exchange letters or e-mail about your schools. Adults can find a school for children to correspond with by going to Intercultural E-mail Classroom Connections at *www.iecc.org*.

**Books in other chapters that also explore the themes of Going to School:**

*The Art Lesson* by Tomie de Paola. Chap. 6 (P)

*Book* by George Ella Lyon. Chap. 10 (P, I)

*Cuban Kids* by George Ancona. Chap. 5 (I)

*Deshawn Days* by Tony Medina. Chap. 4 (I, U)

*Gooney Bird Greene* by Lois Lowry. Chap. 10 (I)

*Gus and Grandpa and Show-and-Tell* by Claudia Mills. Chap. 1 (I)

*Home at Last* by Susan Middletown Elya. Chap. 5 (P, I)

*Hoot* by Carl Hiassen. Chap. 9 (U)

*A Hundred Dresses* by Eleanor Estes. Chap. 3 (I)

*Judy Moody* by Megan McDonald. Chap. 3 (I)

*Judy Moody Saves the World* by Megan McDonald. Chap. 9 (I)

*Junie B., First Grader (at Last!)* by Barbara Park. Chap. 3 (I)

*Just Juice* by Karen Hesse. Chap. 8 (U)

*The Landry News* by Andrew Clement. Chap. 6 (U)

*Little Wolf's Book of Badness* by Ian Whybrow. Chap. 7 (I)

*Minerva Louise at School* by Janet Stoeke. Chap. 7 (P)

*Nothing Ever Happens on 90th Street* by Roni Schotter. Chap. 10 (I)

*Olivia Joins the Circus* by Ian Falconer. Chap. 10 (P)

*Once Upon a Time* by Niki Daly. Chap. 8 (P)

*On the Town: A Community Adventure* by Judith Caseley. Chap. 4 (P)

*Out of Darkness: The Story of Louis Braille* by Russell Freedman. Chap. 9 (I, U)

*Owen* by Kevin Henkes. Chap. 1 (P)

*Ramona Quimby, Age 8* by Beverly Cleary. Chap. 6 (I)

*Sector 7* by David Wiesner. Chap. 10 (P)

*Skinnybones* by Barbara Park. Chap. 7 (I, U)

*The Story of Ruby Bridges* by Robert Coles. Chap. 9 (I)

*Summer Reading Is Killing Me* by Jon Sciezska. Chap. 7 (I)

*Trout and Me* by Susan Shreve. Chap. 3 (U)

*Wolf!* by Becky Bloom. Chap. 7 (P)

## CHAPTER 3: Making Friends

*What is a friend? How do you make and keep friends?*

Making friends is a lifelong process and many of the books on this list include friends and friendship issues. In fact, most of the books annotated here feature some sort of friendship. So anything you read from this list with a child may deal with such topics as: how to be a good friend; friendly gestures and actions; making and losing a friend; tolerating a friend's quirks; inter-generational friendships; the companionship of an animal friend; what friends do together; making up and apologizing; and cross-cultural friendships.

*Some ideas to get you started:*

• Choose a book in which people who might be friends face a challenge or problem, like *Chester's Way*, *Gold Dust*, *The Jacket* or *Surviving Brick Johnson*. Pretend you're one of the friends and write or tell of your feelings about the other person. You might comment on two parts of the story: when you first met your friend and later at the end of the story. How did you and your friendship change?

• Read some of the stories about having a pet, such as *The Stray Dog*, *Henry and Mudge in the Family Trees*, *Shiloh*, or *The Broken Cat*. Then tell or write about a story of a pet you know or a pet you wish you had.

• Make a "me" collage, as Judy did in *Judy Moody Saves the World*, only make it for a friend. Get started by listing all of the things your friend likes and words that might describe the friend. Then look through magazines, choose scraps of fabric, cut up photographs (with permission!), and include anything that would symbolize this friend's personality and interests. This would be even more fun to do with a friend, and then you could trade collage pictures.

• Ask two adults to tell you about their oldest friend. Why have they stayed friends so long? Has their friendship changed?

**Books in other chapters that also explore the themes of Making Friends:**

*Arthur for the Very First Time* by Patricia MacLachlan. Chap. 6 (I, U)

*Because of Winn-Dixie* by Kate DiCamillo. Chap. 4 (I, U)

*Boundless Grace* by Mary Hoffman. Chap. 1 (P, I)

*Bud, Not Buddy* by Christopher Paul Curtis. Chap. 6 (U)

*Chicken Sunday* by Patricia Polacco. Chap. 4 (P)

*Class President* by Johanna Hurwitz. Chap. 2 (U)

*Cool Crazy Crickets to the Rescue!* by David Elliott. Chap. 9 (I)

*Crispin: The Cross of Lead* by Avi. Chap. 6 (U)

*Feather Boy* by Nick Singer. Chap. 6 (U)

*How Tiá Lola Came to Visit/Stay* by Julia Alvarez. Chap. 1 (U)

*Iris and Walter: The School Play* by Elissa Haden Guest. Chap. 8 (P)

*The Jacket* by Andrew Clement. Chap. 9 (U)

*Love, Ruby Lavender* by Deborah Wiles. Chap. 1 (U)

*My Name is Jorge: On Both Sides of the River* by Jane Medina. Chap. 2 (I, U)

*The Name Jar* by Yangsook Choi. Chap. 2 (P, I)

*The Recess Queen* by Alexis O'Neil. Chap. 2 (P)

*Ruby Holler* by Sharon Creech. Chap. 6 (U)

*Saffy's Angel* by Hilary McKay. Chap. 1 (U)

*Seed Folks* by Paul Fleischman. Chap. 9 (U)

*Surviving Brick Johnson* by Laurie Myers. Chap. 2 (U)

*Talkin' About Bessie: The Story of Aviator Elizabeth Coleman* by Nikki Grimes. Chap. 9 (I, U)

*Weslandia* by Paul Fleischman. Chap. 10 (I)

*Yoko* by Rosemary Wells. Chap. 2 (P)

*Yo! Yes?* by Chris Raschka. Chap. 9 (P, I)

# CHAPTER 4: Connecting to Communities

*What makes a community? What communities are you a part of?* While everyone lives in some sort of community, we participate in many, whether it's a neighborhood, town, club, classroom, recreation center, or culture. Books in this chapter touch on these themes: viewing a community and how it works; who is in a community; mapping; comparing urban and rural life; being a part of more than one community or culture; improving or rehabilitating a place or building; services and occupations in a community; overcoming community problems; how communities change over time.

*Some ideas to get you started:*

• Invite people from your local government or community service program to talk about their jobs and why they chose them. Or, visit a city service site, such as the water plant, the bus garage, the sewer treatment plant, or the town hall to see what goes on there.

• Look at a book in which walls of a building are decorated, such as *Barrio: José's Neighborhood*, *Gugu's House*, or *The Little Painter of Sabana Grande*. Then make a wall mural for your room, classroom, or other large area. Work on big paper to plan what your design will look like. Decide with adults whether you'll paint the paper and mount it on the wall or paint directly on the wall.

• Do a little research on an old building in your community. Who lived there? Who built it? When? What was it used for? See if you can locate an old photograph of the building. What details can you see that reveal the building's history, such as faint signs on a brick wall, old-fashioned flowers, fancy carvings above the doorway, or unusual windows or wrought iron railings. You might start with the library, local historical society, town hall, or a neighbor who has lived in your community for a long time.

• Read a book about community activism, such as *Seed Folks*, *Edwina Victorious*, or *Music, Music for Everyone*. What does your community need to make it better? Make a list of your discoveries. Then choose one and begin to do something to help.

• Look in the yellow pages of your phone book and see what you can find out about services in your town. How many banks, gas stations, garden centers, restaurants, plumbers, or some other category can you count? Show your findings on a graph so you can tell others what you discovered.

**Books in other chapters that also explore the themes of Connecting to Communities:**

*Bud, Not Buddy* by Christopher Paul Curtis. Chap. 6 (U)

*A Chair for My Mother* by Vera B. Williams. Chap. 1 (P)

*Chang and the Bamboo Flute* by Elizabeth Starr Hill. Chap. 6 (I)

*Georgie Lee* by Sharon Phillips Denslow. Chap. 1 (I, U)

*How Tiá Lola Came to Visit/Stay* by Julia Alvarez. Chap. 1 (U)

*If the World Were a Village: A Book about the World's People* by David J. Smith. Chap. 5 (U)

*Just Like Home/Como en Mi Tierra* by Elizabeth I. Miller. Chap. 5 (P)

*Love, Ruby Lavender* by Deborah Wiles. Chap. 1 (U)

*Market!* by Ted Lewin. Chap. 5 (I).

*The Most Beautiful Place in the World* by Ann Cameron. Chap. 5 (I, U)

*My Chinatown: One Year in Poems* by Kam Mak. Chap. 5 (I, U)

*Number the Stars* by Lois Lowry. Chap. 3 (I, U)

*The Secret School* by Avi. Chap. 2 (U)

*Seed Folks* by Paul Fleischman. Chap. 9 (U).

*Smoky Night* by Eve Bunting. Chap. 8 (P, I)

*Song of the Trees* by Mildred Taylor. Chap. 1 (I)

*Storm Warriors* by Elisa Carbone. Chap. 6 (U)

*The Storytellers* by Ted Lewin. Chap. 1 (P)

*Vejigante Masquerader* by Lulu Delacre. Chap. 5 (P, I)

*When the Circus Came to Town* by Laurence Yep. Chap. 3 (I, U)

*The Year of Miss Agnes* by Kirkpatrick Hill. Chap. 2 (U)

## CHAPTER 5: Looking at the World

*How are people alike the world over? How are they different?*
Children can see we live in a world that links and intertwines. Books in this chapter seek to present authentic views of many cultures and include these themes: contemporary life in other countries; contemporary life for immigrants to the United States; similarities and differences in family, food, school, or friendships across cultures; art in culture; adjusting to change; the importance of literacy; the impact of political unrest on families; living in two cultures; the effect of geography on culture; marveling at the earth's diversity of people and land; preserving the earth.

*Some ideas to get you started:*

- Find a large world map. Read some books set in other countries and locate those spots on your map. Good starting places are *Galimoto, Snake Charmer, Cuban Kids, The Pot That Juan Built,* and *Chang and the Bamboo Flute.* Then, compare the details in the book with what you could predict from the map of that country.

- Investigate a book set in another country for all of the cultural details you notice, either in pictures or in the story, of what people eat, how they dress, what they do in their spare time, jobs parents or children have, and so forth. Then read another book set in that same area to see how the details are similar.

- Talk with people from another culture or country about their childhoods. Prepare questions. Then, share your findings in a picture, or in writing. If you do this with others, make a display of your findings and be sure to locate your person's country of origin on a map.

- Read any of the books on this list and think about how you are similar to the people in your book. Think about how you are different. What do you discover?

**Books in other chapters that also explore the themes of Looking at the World:**

*black is brown is tan* by Arnold Adoff. Chap. 1 (P)

*Boundless Grace* by Mary Hoffman. Chap. 1 (P, I)

*Chang and the Bamboo Flute* by Elizabeth Starr Hill. Chap. 6 (I)

*Dim Sum for Everyone* by Grace Lin. Chap. 1 (P)

*Dream Carver* by Diana Cohn. Chap. 6 (I)

*Frida* by Jonah Winter. Chap 6 (I)

*Galimoto* by Karen Lynn Williams. Chap. 10 (P, I)

*Grandfather's Journey* by Allen Say. Chap. 1 (I)

*Gugu's House* by Catherine Stock. Chap. 10 (P, I)

*My Name is Jorge: On Both Sides of the River* by Jane Medina. Chap. 2 (I, U)

*Out of Darkness: The Story of Louis Braille* by Russell Freedman. Chap. 9 (I, U)

*The Pot That Juan Built* by Nancy Andrews-Goebel. Chap. 10 (P, I)

*Powwow* by George Ancona. Chap. 4 ( I)

*The Storytellers* by Ted Lewin. Chap 1 (P)

*Weslandia* by Paul Fleischman. Chap. 10 (I)

*What's Up, What's Down* by Lola M. Schaefer. Chap. 10 (P)

*When My Name Was Keoko: A Novel of Korea in World War II* by Linda Sue Park. Chap. 10 (U)

*Who Was the Woman Who Wore the Hat?* by Nancy Patz. Chap. 10 (U)

*Willow and Twig* by Jean Little. Chap. 8 (U)

*The Year of Miss Agnes* by Kirkpatrick Hill. Chap. 2 (U)

*Yoko* by Rosemary Wells. Chap. 2 (P)

## CHAPTER 6: Looking in a Mirror

*Who am I? How am I changing?*
Children are so eager to grow up and seek evidence that they're changing. Books in this chapter explore the many ways a person grows, naturally, with influences from others, and with experiences, both good and bad. Themes that might be introduced include the following: accepting yourself and your family; defining yourself; understanding your family or cultural heritage; finding something to do that gives you pleasure and finding an occupation; taking courageous steps; breaking the mold; being true to yourself in spite of setbacks or the opinions of others; dealing with parental expectations; exploring emotions; dealing with physical and emotional differences; tackling new experiences; being hopeful.

## Some ideas to get you started:

- Make a layered timeline of your life. On the top line, include important incidents in your life so far. On separate timelines underneath, you might put key events in the development of your sports skills or hobby; favorite books at various ages; trips you've taken over the years; or key events from any area of your life. Add to this, either by extending timelines or adding another layer.

- Read biographies, such as *America's Champion Swimmer: Gertrude Ederle; Eleanor Roosevelt: A Life of Discovery; Snowflake Bentley; Frida; Frank O. Gehry: Outside In;* or *A Strong Right Arm: The Story of Mamie "Peanut" Johnson*. Talk about or make a list of what obstacles, attitudes of the time, disabilities, or some other issue got in the way of this person and how he or she overcame them.

- Write a letter, an e-mail, or talk to relatives about their childhoods. You might prepare questions about school, entertainment, or family life before you begin to chat. How is your life similar to theirs? Different? Which relative are you most like?

- Find photographs of yourself at various ages and organize them chronologically. Make a book of yourself from your early days to now. You might enjoy putting captions under each photograph telling what's happening or who is in the photo with you. Look at books by Patricia Polacco, such as *My Rotten Red-Headed Older Brother*, to see how she includes family photos in her illustrations, as well.

### Books in other chapters that also explore the themes of Looking in a Mirror:

*black is brown is tan* by Arnold Adoff. Chap. 1 (P)

*Boundless Grace* by Mary Hoffman. Chap. 1 (P, I)

*Brave as a Mountain Lion* by Ann Herbert Scott. Chap. 2 (P, I)

*The Breadwinner* by Deborah Ellis. Chap. 8 (U)

*Cherry Pies and Lullabies* by Lynne Reiser. Chap. 1 (P, I)

*Child of the Owl* by Laurence Yep. Chap. 4 (U)

*Cinder Edna* by Ellen Jackson. Chap. 7 (I)

*Ella Enchanted* by Gail Carson Levine. Chap. 10 (U)

*Flying Solo* by Ralph Fletcher. Chap. 2 (U)

*Frank O. Gehry: Outside In* by Jan Greenberg and Sandra Jordan. Chap. 9 (U)

*Freedom Summer* by Deborah Wiles. Chap. 3 (P, I)

*The Giver* by Lois Lowry. Chap. 4 (U)

*Gold Dust* by Chris Lynch. Chap. 3 (U)

*Grandaddy and Janetta Together: The Three Stories in One Book* by Helen V. Griffith. Chap. 1 (I)

*Hatchet* by Gary Paulsen. Chap. 8 (U)

*The Jacket* by Andrew Clement. Chap. 9 (U)

*Jakarta Missing* by Jane Kurtz. Chap. 5 (U)

*Just Juice* by Karen Hesse. Chap. 8 (U)

*Just Like Home/Como en Mi Tierra* by Elizabeth I. Miller. Chap. 5 (P)

*Love, Ruby Lavender* by Deborah Wiles. Chap. 1 (U)

*Love That Dog* by Sharon Creech. Chap. 2 (I, U)

*The Most Beautiful Place in the World* by Ann Cameron. Chap. 5 (I, U)

*Nadia's Hands* by Karen English. Chap. 5 (I)

*Other Side of Truth* by Beverly Naidoo. Chap. 5 (U)

*Poppy* by Avi. Chap. 8 (I)

*Saffy's Angel* by Hilary McKay. Chap. 1 (U)

*Same Stuff as Stars* by Katherine Paterson. Chap. 1 (U)

*The Secret School* by Avi. Chap. 2 (U)

*The Steps* by Rachel Cohn. Chap. 8 (U)

*Surviving Brick Johnson* by Laurie Myers. Chap. 2 (U)

*Tell Me a Story, Mama* by Angela Johnson. Chap. 1 (P)

*A Week in the Woods* by Andrew Clement. Chap. 2 (U)

*Wemberly Worried* by Kevin Henkes. Chap. 2 (P)

*When the Circus Came to Town* by Laurence Yep. Chap. 3 (I, U)

*Yang the Youngest and His Terrible Ear* by Lensey Namioka. Chap. 1 (I, U)

## CHAPTER 7: Laughing Together

*What makes you chuckle, giggle, laugh?*
Everyone likes to laugh. Beyond having a good time with these books, we think readers might like to explore these concepts: types of humor, such as puns, word play, exaggeration, jokes, situations; spin-offs or parodies of folktales and other well-known stories; how some stories invite writers to tell their own versions; literary devices such as metaphor, alliteration, point of view, allusion, onomatopoeia, and exaggeration.

### Some ideas to get you started:

- Look at the exaggerated humor in books such as *"Could Be Worse!," McBroom's Wonderful One-Acre Farm: Three Tall Tales, And to Think That I Saw It on Mulberry Street, Gooney Bird Greene,* or *The Birdwatchers*. Try spinning your own exaggerated tale of some common activity you do, like riding the bus to school, taking out the trash, or cleaning your room. You could illustrate your story, too.

- Read *How Tom Beat Captain Najork and His Hired Sportsmen* or *Weslandia,* and decide on the rules for one of the games they played in the book. Or invent your own game with a funny purpose or goal and odd rules.

- Have a riddle and joke day and tell each other knock-knocks and other kinds of jokes. You can find many joke collections in magazines, like *Readers' Digest* and *Boy's Life,* as well as riddle and joke books in the library. Maybe your family knows some jokes they tell over and over but your friends have never heard them.

- Serenade someone with one of the silly songs from *Take Me Out of the Bathtub and Other Silly Dilly Songs* or recite a funny poem from *The Frog Wore Red Suspenders*. Put on a show for an audience of friends or classmates.

- Look at the many books that are based on folktales, such as *Cinder Edna*, *If the Shoe Fits: Voices from Cinderella*, *Once Upon a Marigold*, or *The Giant Carrot*. Then tell or write another favorite folktale from a different point of view, or in a new setting such as your school, the soccer field, or the Wild West. Tell or read your story to others see if you can make them laugh.

**Books in other chapters that also explore the themes of Laughing Together:**

*And to Think That I Saw it on Mulberry Street* by Dr. Seuss. Chap. 10 (P, I)

*Attaboy, Sam!* by Lois Lowry. Chap. 1 (I, U)

*The Birdwatchers* by Simon James. Chap. 10 (P)

*Bunnicula: A Rabbit Tale of Mystery* by Deborah and James Howe. Chap. (I, U)

*Duck on a Bike* by David Shannon. Chap. 10 (P)

*First Graders from Mars: Horus's Horrible Day* by Shana Corey. Chap. 2 (P)

*George and Martha* by James Marshall. Chapter 3 (P)

*The Giant Carrot* by Jan Peck. Chap. 4 (P)

*Gooney Bird Greene* by Lois Lowry. Chapter 10 (I)

*Harley* by Star Livingston. Chap. 3 (P, I)

*Hey, Kid, Want to Buy a Bridge?* by Jon Scieszka. Chap. 10 (I)

*Holes* by Louis Sachar. Chap. 3 (U)

*How Ben Franklin Stole the Lightning* by Rosalyn Schanzer. Chap. 10 (I, U)

*If You're Not Here, Please Raise Your Hand: Poems about School* by Kalli Dakos. Chap. 2 (I, U)

*Judy Moody* by Megan McDonald. Chap. 3 (I)

*Junie B. Jones, First Grader (at Last!)* by Barbara Park. Chap. 3 (I)

*The Know Nothings* by Michele Sobel Spirn. Chap. 3 (P)

*Mud Flat Spring* by James Stevenson. Chap. 3 (P, I)

*Olivia Joins the Circus* by Ian Falconer. Chap. 10 (P)

*Pete's a Pizza* by William Steig. Chap. 1 (P).

*See You Around, Sam* by Lois Lowry. Chap. 4 (I)

*26 Fairmont Street* by Tomie de Paola. Chapter 1 (P, I)

## CHAPTER 8: Getting Through Tough Times

*What qualities get people through tough times?*
*How might you help someone who is having difficulties?*
Maybe there are some lucky people who never go through a difficult time in their lives but we don't know any. Readers can discover the following themes in the books on this list: coping with fears; reaching out to another person; hardships faced in history; dealing with grief or death; developing emotional awareness; learning to talk about feelings; developing perseverance, patience, and hope; people who can help; transforming despair into action; the role of stories and storytelling in overcoming fear; recognizing your own inner strengths.

*Some ideas to get you started:*

- Choose a character from one of the stories on this list, like the title characters in *Amber Was Brave, Essie Was Smart*; the girl in *Flamingo Dream* who has lost her father; or Austin in *Blackberries in the Dark*, who has lost his grandfather. Jump ahead five or 10 years and tell how this boy or girl now remembers those times and in what ways the character is stronger.

- Find a newspaper article that tells of someone having a hard time. Who is helping that person? Be sure to look for support from city services, family and friends, church, club, or other community groups. Or, tell how an organization you belong to helps people who are having difficulties.

- People in *Marvin One Too Many*, *Just Juice*, and *Once Upon a Time* have a hard time learning to read. How do they overcome their difficulty? Who helps? What kinds of things make reading harder? What makes reading easier? What advice can you give to someone struggling with reading?

- Invite an adult who has lived through the Great Depression, World War II, or some other national hard time, to talk about that period in history. Prepare some questions, such as what was it difficult to get, and what did you have to do differently as a result.

- Read *The Breadwinner*, a novel set in modern Afghanistan. What were some struggles Afghanis had engaged in before the book began? What difficulties do people face in this story? What do they hope for? Locate news stories and find out what's currently happening in this country. Read novels set in other countries and use this same approach to see what you can learn about a place, the people who live there, and history.

**Books in other chapters that also explore the themes of Getting Through Tough Times:**

*Because of Winn-Dixie* by Kate DiCamillo. Chap. 4 (I, U)

*Bud, Not Buddy* by Christopher Paul Curtis. Chap. 6 (U)

*Bridge to Terebithia* by Katherine Paterson. Chap. 3 (U)

*A Chair for My Mother* by Vera B. Williams. Chap. 1 (P)

*Chang and the Bamboo Flute* by Elizabeth Starr Hill. Chap. 6 (I)

*Charlotte's Web* by E.B. White. Chap. 3 (I, U)

*Crispin: The Cross of Lead* by Avi. Chap. 6 (U)

*Esperanza Rising* by Pam Muñoz Ryan. Chap. 4 (U)

*Feather Boy* by Nick Singer. Chap. 6 (U)

*Fig Pudding* by Ralph Fletcher. Chap. 1 (U)

*Fireboat: The Heroic Adventures of John J. Harvey* by Maira Kalman. Chap. 4 (P, I)

*Freak the Mighty* by Rodman Philbrick. Chap. 3 (U)

*The Gardener* by Sarah Stewart. Chap. 6 (I)

*Gettin' Through Thursday* by Melrose Cooper. Chap. 1 (P)

*Good Night, Mr. Tom* by Michelle Magorian. Chap. 3 (U)

*Grandpa's Corner Store* by Dyanne DiSalvo-Ryan. Chap. 4 (I)

*Jakarta Missing* by Jane Kurtz. Chap. 5 (U)

*Little Rat Sets Sail* by Monica Bang-Campbell. Chap. 6 (P, I)

*Love That Dog* by Sharon Creech. Chap. 2 (I, U)

*Marianthe's Story: Painted Words/Spoken Memories* by Aliki. Chap. 2 (P, I, U)

*Mary on Horseback: The Three Mountain Stories* by Rosemary Wells. Chap. 9 (U)

*Matthew and Tilly* by Rebecca Jones. Chap. 3 (P)

*Mick Harte Was Here* by Barbara Park. Chap. 6 (U)

*The Most Beautiful Place in the World* by Ann Cameron. Chap. 5 (I, U)

*My Louisiana Sky* by Kimberly Willis Holt. Chap. 3 (U)

*Other Side of Truth* by Beverly Naidoo. Chap. 5 (U)

*The Rough-Face Girl* by Rafe Martin. Chap. 6 (P, I)

*Ruby Holler* by Sharon Creech. Chap. 6 (U)

*Same Stuff as Stars* by Katherine Paterson. Chap. 1 (U)

*Seed Folks* by Paul Fleischman. Chap. 9 (U)

*Surviving Brick Johnson* by Laurie Myers. Chap. 2 (U)

*Uncle Jed's Barbershop* by Margaree King Mitchell. Chap. 4 (I)

*Under the Mango Tree* by Amy Bronwen Zemser. Chap. 5 (U)

*The Watsons Go to Birmingham–1963* by Christopher Paul Curtis. Chap. 1 (U)

*When the Circus Came to Town* by Laurence Yep. Chap. 3 (I, U)

*Where I'd Like to Be* by Frances O'Roark Dowell. Chap. 6 (U)

*Wilma Unlimited: How Wilma Rudolph Became the World's Fastest Woman* by Katherine Krull. Chap. 6 (P, I)

## CHAPTER 9: Making a Difference

*How do kids make a difference? What can I do to help?*
Most people would like to help others in need but they often don't know how. Books in this chapter encourage children to think about these ideas: volunteering or showing up to help; investigating appropriate action in the community; standing up for principles; writing letters; exploring civil rights; making good choices; occupations that help foster change; and biographies of people who were catalysts for change in history.

*Some ideas to get you started:*
• Visit someone. Beforehand, you could cook something, like the cake from the recipe in *Thunder Cake* or "The Pudding Like a Night from the Sea" in *The Stories Julian Tells*. (You can find the recipe on author Ann Cameron's Web site, *www.childrensbestbooks.com*) Then, share your cake or pudding with someone who may need cheering up.

• Read *The Castle on Viola Street* or *Seed Folks*. Ask someone to come and talk to you about house rehabilitation or garden opportunities in your community. How can children help? Or, find newspaper or magazine articles about ways people help beautify or improve their communities. Find out what civic, religious, or city groups have public service as a part of their organization.

• Read *Miss Rumphius* or *Something Beautiful*. Make a list of things that could use a little improvement, like trash pick-up in your neighborhood, some flowers in front of a sign, or a new coat of paint on the community center shed. See if an adult will help you organize an event so that others can contribute their time and efforts, too. Or, invite Eagle Scouts or Girl Scouts who have earned the Gold Award to talk to you about their community service projects, what they did, and how they organized them.

• Make a wall of heroes, people you admire who did something to help others. Find a picture, or make one, and write a small description of what these heroes did. If you do this with others, plan your display to look interesting. You might include a timeline and put your people near the dates when they were heroic. Do something yourself and put your own picture up there with a description of what you did.

• Read *Silver Packages: An Appalachian Christmas Story*. To learn more about the Santa Train, contact *www.kingsportchamber.org*. Perhaps you and others would like to send (before November) a box of small gifts, like a new book, socks, or a child's toy, to be included in the annual Christmas train run.

**Books in other chapters that also explore the themes of Making a Difference:**

*Arthur for the Very First Time* by Patricia MacLachlan. Chap. 6 (I, U)

*Boundless Grace* by Mary Hoffman. Chap. 1 (P, I)

*Chang and the Bamboo Flute* by Elizabeth Starr Hill. Chap 6 (I)

*Chato and the Party Animals* by Gary Soto. Chap. 4 (P)

*Dear Whiskers* by Ann Whitehead Nagda. Chap. 2 (I)

*The Dinosaurs of Waterhouse Hawkins* by Barbara Kerley. Chap. 10 (I, U)

*Eleanor Roosevelt: A Life of Discovery* by Russell Freedman. Chap. 6 (U)

*Fireboat: The Heroic Adventures of the John J. Harvey* by Maira Kalman. Chap. 4 (P, I)

*Flying Solo* by Ralph Fletcher. Chap. 2 (U)

*The Four Ugly Cats in Apartment 3D* by Marilyn Sachs. Chap. 4 (I)

*Freak the Mighty* by Rodman Philbrick. Chap. 3 (U)

*The Gardener* by Sarah Stewart. Chap. 6 (I)

*Girls Think of Everything: Stories of Ingenious Inventions by Women* by Catherine Thimmesh. Chap. 10 (I, U)

*Grandfather's Journey* by Allen Say. Chap. 1 (I)

*Grandpa's Corner Store* by Dyanne DiSalvo-Ryan. Chap. 4 (I)

*Henry and Mudge and the Happy Cat* by Cynthia Rylant. Chap. 6 (P)

*Jamaica and the Substitute Teacher* by Juanita Havill. Chap 2 (P)

*The Most Beautiful Place in the World* by Ann Cameron. Chap. 5 (I, U)

*Not My Dog* by Colby Rodowsky. Chap. 6 (I)

*Owen Foote, Money Man* by Stephanie Greene. Chap. 1 (I)

*The Pot That Juan Built* by Nancy Andrews-Goebel. Chap. 10 (P, I)

*Raising Yoder's Barn* by Jane Yolen. Chap. 4 (P, I)

*Teammates* by Peter Golenbock. Chap. 3 (I)

*Thank You, Mr. Falker* by Patricia Polacco. Chap. 2 (P, I)

*Uncle Jed's Barbershop* by Margaree King Mitchell. Chap. 4 (I)

*The Year of Miss Agnes* by Kirkpatrick Hill. Chap. 2 (U)

## CHAPTER 10: Exploring Imagination

*How is imagination useful? How can you take your imagination out for a spin?*

Children have brilliant imaginations but they sometimes need inspiration. Books on this list help readers explore these concepts: different kinds of creativity; the role of art, reading, and writing in developing creativity; groundbreaking visual formats; thinking outside the box; making something from nothing; imagining future or other worlds; playing with conventions such as ABC books, concrete poetry, cartoons, or biographies; conveying information in unconventional ways; the impact of imaginative people on our lives; surprises; models for writing.

*Some ideas to get you started:*

• Children in *Roxaboxen; Cool, Crazy Crickets to the Rescue!;* and *Where I'd Like to Be* made play towns, club houses, or other interesting spots in which to play. Make your own spot with some friends and furnish it imaginatively. Have a picnic in your spot.

• Check out some of the many alphabet books listed, such as those in *Alphabet Under Construction*, or others you find in the library. Decide how the author organized the book: Is it themed? Does it try to teach? Does it use alliteration or a story? Then, write your own alphabet book, perhaps using words from a sport, information about a country, or alliteration. Ask someone else to read your new book.

• Look at some great paintings, such as an abstract one from *Action Jackson* or a more representational one. You could visit a museum or use art books from the library. Imagine you walked into that painting or the subjects in that painting climbed down off the wall for an adventure. What happens next? Write or tell a story and share it with someone.

• Chris Van Allsburg's books always include interesting "what if" ideas. Get as many of his books as you can find, read them, and talk about the imaginative possibilities that underpin his stories. What if ants had an adventure in the kitchen? What if a boy visited the North Pole to see Santa? What if Jack Frost lost his way in the fall? Try your hand at writing your own "what if" story.

• Pick a scene from a favorite story and see how many different kinds of art you can use to portray it. Try collage from magazines, wrapping paper, and other materials. Then try paints, both watercolor and some other sort. Make scratchboard by coloring hard with a crayon on white paper, then covering the crayon with India ink or black paint before scratching your illustration in it. You might use clay, Play-Doh, or Sculpey on flat cardboard for your next illustration. What medium was most fun? Most messy? Best for your illustration? When you read a picture book, see if you can find out what kind of art the illustrator used.

### Books in other chapters that also explore the themes of Exploring Imagination:

*The Art Lesson* by Tomie de Paola. Chap. 6 (P)

*Brown Angels* by Walter Dean Myers. Chap. 1 (P, I)

*Dream Carver* by Diana Cohn. Chap. 6 (I)

*Frank O. Gehry: Outside In* by Jan Greenberg and Sandra Jordan. Chap. 9 (U)

*Frida* by Jonah Winter. Chap. 6 (I)

*Frindle* by Andrew Clement. Chap. 2 (U).

*Gettin' Through Thursday* by Melrose Cooper. Chap. 1 (P)

*Go Away, Big Green Monster* by Ed Emberley. Chap. 8 (P)

*How Tom Beat Captain Najork and His Hired Sportsmen* by Russell Hoban. Chap. 7 (I)

*A Hundred Dresses* by Eleanor Estes. Chap. 3 (I)

*I'll Meet You at the Cucumbers* by Lilian Moore. Chap. 4 (I)

*The Little Painter of Sabana Grande* by Patricia Maloney Markun. Chap. 4 (P)

*Math Curse* by Jon Scieszka and Lane Smith. Chap. 2 (U)

*Pete's a Pizza* by William Steig. Chap. 1 (P)

*The Real, True Dulcie Campbell* by Cynthia DeFelice. Chap. 6 (P)

*Tornado* by Betsy Byars. Chap. 8 (I)

*When the Circus Came to Town* by Laurence Yep. Chap. 3 (I, U)

# Additional Resources

This is just a starter list! Follow the leads these books, Web sites, and organizations provide you.

## Books about children's literature, their creators, and ways to make books come alive

Cart, Michael. 1995. *What's So Funny?: Wit and Humor in American Children's Literature*. New York, NY: HarperCollins.

Cummings, Patricia. 1992. *Talking With Artists: Conversations with Victoria Chess, Pat Cummings, Leo and Diane Dillon, Richard Egielski, Lois Ehlert, Lisa Campbell Ernst, Tom Feelings, Steven Kellogg, Jerry Pinkney, Amy Schwartz, Lane Smith, Chris Van Allsburg, and David Wiesner*. New York, NY: Simon & Schuster.

———. 1995. *Talking With Artists, Volume 2: Conversations with Thomas B. Allen, Mary Jane Begin, Floyd Cooper, Julie Downing, Denise Fleming, Sheila Hamanaka, Kevin Henkes, William Joyce, Maira Kalman, Deborah Nourse Lattimore, Brian Pinkney, Vera B. Williams, and David Wisniewski*. New York, NY: Simon & Schuster.

———. 1999. *Talking With Artists, Volume 3: Conversations with Peter Catalanotto, Rául Colón, Lisa Desimini, Jane Dyer, Kevin Hawkes, G. Brian Karas, Betsy Lewin, Ted Lewin, Keiko Narahashi, Elise Primavera, Anna Rich, Peter Sís, and Paul O. Zelinsky*. New York, NY: Houghton Mifflin.

Daniels, Harvey. 2002. *Literature Circles: Voice and Choice in Book Clubs & Reading Groups*, 2nd ed. Portland, ME: Stenhouse.

Dodson, Shireen. 1997. *The Mother/Daughter Book Club: How Ten Busy Mothers and Daughters Came Together to Talk, Laugh and Learn Through Their Love of Reading*. New York, NY: Perennial.

Dresang, Eliza. 1999. *Radical Change: Books for Youth in a Digital Age*. Bronx, NY: H.W. Wilson.

Huck, Charlotte, Barbara Kiefer, Susan Hepler, Janet Hickman. 2004. *Children's Literature in the Elementary School*, 8th ed. New York, NY: McGraw-Hill.

Kristo, Janice.V., and Rosemary Bamford, eds. 2003. *Making Facts Come Alive: Choosing Quality Nonfiction Literature K-8*, 2nd ed. Norwood, MA: Christopher-Gordon.

Peterson, Ralph, and Maryann Eeds. 1990. *Grand Conversations: Literature Groups in Action*. New York, NY: Scholastic Educational Paperbacks.

Routman, Regie. 2003. *Reading Essentials: The Specifics You Need To Teach Reading Well*. Portsmouth, NH: Heinemann.

Silvey, Anita. 1995. *Children's Books and Their Creators*. Boston, MA: Houghton Mifflin.

———. 2002. *The Essential Guide to Children's Books and Their Creators*. Boston, MA: Houghton Mifflin.

## Useful Web sites and organizations

*American Library Association* at www.ala.org. Find lists of books recommended by librarians from across the country such as the Newbery and Caldecott Medal and honor books, Notable Children's Books, Coretta Scott King Award winners and honor books, and the Pura Belpré Award winners and honor books. Link to other sites especially for parents and find out more about recommended Web sites for children here, too.

*Capitol Choices: Noteworthy Books for Children* found at www.capitolchoices.org. Find new books recommended by teachers, librarians, booksellers, and other children's literature specialists. Visit this Web site to "listen in" as 100 current books are discussed online to identify 100 of the year's best.

*Children's Book Council (CBC)* at www.cbcbooks.org. Learn more about popular authors and illustrators, find out what awards are given to children's books, learn about writing, illustrating, and publishing children's books. Get ideas about celebrating Poetry Week and Children's Book Week and more!

*International Reading Association (IRA)* at www.reading.org. IRA has many resources for teachers and other concerned adults. Visit their site to find out more about IRA publications, other resources, and awards.

*National Council of Teachers of English (NCTE)* at www.ncte.org. NCTE has many resources for teachers and other concerned adults. Visit their site to find out more about NCTE publications, other resources, and links to other relevant Web sites.

*National Education Association (NEA)* at www.nea.org. NEA sponsors Read Across America and other programs that motivate children to read. NEA also has online summaries of research, teaching activities, resources, news, and other Web links related to reading.

*Reading Is Fundamental, Inc. (RIF)* at www.rif.org. RIF offers advice about reading, ways parents and educators can motivate kids to read, and a listing of local RIF program coordinators.

*Reading Rockets* at www.readingrockets.org. Find out the latest news from experts about reading—for adults who live and work with children from birth through nine years. Also, see and hear author interviews and get topical booklists. Reading Rockets developed a related site for PBS at www.pbs.org/launchingreaders.

# Index